They Who Fought Here

They Who Fought Here

Text by BELL IRVIN WILEY

Illustrations selected by HIRST D. MILHOLLEN

Bonanza Books · New York

This edition published by Bonanza Books,
a division of Crown Publishers, Inc.,
by arrangement with The Macmillan Company
b c d e f g h

Printed in the United States of America
Library of Congress catalog card no.: 59–11458

Permission to quote copyright material is gratefully acknowledged to publishers and authors
as follows: The Atlantic Monthly Press—
Meade's Headquarters, 1863–1865, by Colonel
Theodore Lyman, copyright, 1912, by the
Massachusetts Historical Society, for the quotations on pages 67 and 263; Garrett and Mas-
sie, Richmond, Va.—*The University Greys:
Company A, Eleventh Mississippi Regiment,
1861–1865* by Maud Morrow Brown (1940),
for the quotation on page 264; The Macmillan
Company—*Lincoln Finds a General,* Volume I,
by Kenneth P. Williams, copyright, 1949, by
Kenneth P. Williams, for the quotations on
pages 17 and 242; Charles Scribner's Sons—
Military Memoirs of a Confederate by E. P.
Alexander, copyright, 1907, by Charles Scribner's Sons, for the quotation on p. 1; The University of California Press—*The Road to Richmond: The Civil War Memoirs of Major Abner
R. Small of the Sixteenth Maine Volunteers* by
Harold Adams Small (1939) on page 264.

Acknowledgments

The following historical societies, libraries, museums and institutions have contributed pictorial material for this work which is gratefully acknowledged:

Chicago Historical Society, Chicago, Illinois (Mr. Paul M. Angle); Confederate Museum, Charleston, South Carolina (Miss Marie Millings); Confederate Museum, Richmond, Virginia; Detroit Public Library, Detroit, Michigan (Mr. James Babcock); Georgia State Department of Archives and History, Atlanta, Georgia (Mrs. Mary Bryan and Mrs. Ruby F. Thomas); Fredericksburg and Spotsylvania National Military Park, Fredericksburg, Virginia (Mr. Albert Dillahunty, Mr. Ralph Happel and Mr. Robert L. Hilldrup); Illinois State Historical Library, Springfield, Illinois (Mrs. Margaret A. Flint and Mr. Clyde C. Walton); Harvard College Library, Cambridge, Massachusetts (Mr. William A. Jackson and Miss Carolyn Jakeman); The Library of Congress, Washington, D. C. (Dr. Edgar Breitenbach, Mr. Milton Kaplan, Mr. Carl Stange and Dr. C. Percy Powell); Manassas National Battlefield Park, Manassas, Virginia (Mr. Robert G. Sanner and Mr. Francis F. Wilshin); Missouri Historical Society, St. Louis, Missouri (Mrs. Marjory Douglass and Miss Ruth Field); The National Archives, Washington, D.C. (Miss Josephine Cobb, Mr. Julio Perez and Mr. Elmer O. Parker); Smithsonian Institution, Washington, D.C.; West Point Museum, United States Military Academy, West Point, New York (Mr. Richard E. Kuehne).

The generous help of the following is acknowledged:

Dr. John Miller, Office of the Chief of Military History, Department of the Army, for reading and criticizing Chapter 10; Mr. John R. Schneid of Baltimore, Mr. L. Van Loan Naisawald of the Manassas National Battlefield Park, and Craddock Goins, Jr., of the Smithsonian Institution, for reading Chapter 5 and making helpful comments about the content; Professor Robert V. Bruce of Malden, Massachusetts, Mr. Charles A. Collier and Mr. Beverly M. DuBose, Jr., of Atlanta, General Carl A. Baehr of Chevy Chase, Maryland, and Mr. Milton F. Perry of Independence, Missouri, for valuable data on arms and equipment; Mr. Edward Steere of Arlington, Virginia, for making available his unpublished study on the

Wilderness campaign and giving information about logistics; Major John Goodlett, Jr., of the Quartermaster Corps and Mr. Charles F. Romanus of the Office of the Chief of Military History, for running down information about uniforms and clothing; Miss Ruth Walling and Mr. David Estes of the Reference Department, Emory University Library, for helping to find answers to many puzzling questions that arose during the preparation of the narrative.

Mr. Monroe F. Cockrell of Evanston, Illinois, for calling attention to, and permitting quotation of, a choice comment in an unpublished Civil War letter; Charles A. Porter Hopkins and the Maryland Historical Society for permission to use the letters of George F. West; Stephen E. Ambrose of Madison, Wisconsin, for providing a splendid excerpt from the war letters of James K. Newton.

Miss Josephine Cobb, Archivist-in-charge of the Still Picture Branch, the National Archives, for her stimulating advice and encouragement, and her efficient staff: Mr. Harry Bauda, Mrs. Ruth King, Miss Josephine Motylewski and Mr. Joe Thomas. Mr. Donald Holmes, Chief of the Photoduplication Service, the Library of Congress and the following members of his capable staff: Mr. Edward J. Brocious, Mrs. Virginia Brooks, Mr. William Davis, Miss Olivera Durgy, Mr. James Furtwengle, Mrs. Ernestine B. Jacobs and Mr. Elmer King. Without their skill and patience, it would have been impossible to reproduce many of the pictures used. Miss India Thomas, House Regent, and Miss Eleanor Brockenbrough, Assistant House Regent, Confederate Museum, Richmond, Virginia, and Mrs. Ralph Catterall, Librarian, the Valentine Museum, Richmond, Virginia, gave generously of their time and energy and took a special interest in this work. Mr. Edgar Howell, Curator, Military History, Smithsonian Institution, and Mr. Albert Dillahunty and Mr. Ralph Happel, Historians, Fredericksburg and Spotsylvania National Military Park, were most helpful in identification and arranging for photographing of Civil War relics in their custody. Mr. John L. Rawls, Vienna, Virginia, for his kindness in permitting reproduction of certain rare Civil War relics in his fine collection. Mr. and Mrs. Edgar Cox, Falls Church, Virginia, for granting permission for the reproduction of photographs in the Brady-Handy Collection in the Library of Congress. Judge William Finley, Falls Church, Virginia, whose knowledge of photography and assistance in photographing Civil War relics was invaluable.

Among others to whom the authors are deeply indebted are: Mr. Ben Belchic, Winchester, Virginia; Mr. Milton T. Chambers, Baltimore, Maryland; Mrs. Linda Cudé, Washington, D.C.; Dr. Llerena B. Friend, Austin, Texas; Mr. Lee Grove, Pearl River, New York; Mr. Francis C. Haber, Baltimore, Maryland; Dr. Lois Hartly, Rices Landing, Pennsylvania; Miss Bertha L. Heilbron, St. Paul, Minnesota; Mrs. Mabel Hickaby, Austin, Texas; Colonel G. B. Jarrett, Aberdeen, Maryland; Mrs. Varina R. Jones, Alexandria, Virginia; Mr. Virgil C. Jones, Centreville, Virginia; Mrs. McCook Knox, Washington, D.C.; Mrs. J. S. Land, Columbia, South Carolina; Mrs. Virginia Lee, Washington, D.C.; Mr. Harold Lessen, Baltimore, Maryland; Mr. Blakeley Lodge, Philomont, Virginia; Mr. Rex B. Magee, Arlington, Virginia; Dr. Lamar McMillin, Little Rock, Arkansas; Mrs. June Marshall, Washington, D.C.; Mr. Philip P. Mason, Detroit, Michigan; Mr. John E. Meyer, Birmingham, Alabama; Dr. and Mrs. Daniel B. Moffett, Washington, D.C.; Mr. Elmer O. Parker, Washington, D.C.; Mr. John R. Peacock, High Point, North Carolina; Mrs. Garnet Petersen, San Antonio, Texas; Mr. Harold Petersen, Arlington, Virginia; Col. Thomas Spencer, Atlanta, Georgia; Mr. Ezra J. Warner, La Jolla, California; Dr. S. Harrison Williams, Alexandria, Virginia; Mr. Landon Wynkoop, Leesburg, Virginia.

Contents

I   THE OPPOSING FORCES   1

II   "JOINING UP"   19

III   RATIONS   47

IV   CLOTHING AND SHELTER   67

V   WEAPONS   101

VI   DIVERSIONS   141

VII   CRIME AND PUNISHMENT   163

VIII   MORALS AND RELIGION   187

IX   THE SICK AND WOUNDED   207

X   "PASS THE INFANTRY TO THE FRONT"   239

PICTURE CREDITS   271

They Who Fought Here

The Opposing Forces

"The camps near the principal Northern towns were all of regiments. Those in the South were mostly of a company each. The arms of the Northern troops were generally the long-range rifled muskets. Those of the Southern troops were almost universally the old-fashioned, smooth-bore muskets. The Northern troops were always neatly uniformed in blue, their camps seemed well equipped, and there was generally some visible show of military discipline about them. The Confederate uniforms were blue, gray, or brown, and sometimes uniforms were lacking. There was, too, a noticeable contrast in the physical appearance of the men, the Northern and Western men having more flesh and better color. As physical machines, to withstand hardships, a casual observer would have pronounced them superior to their antagonists. But I lived to see that appearances may deceive. Indeed, it became a never-ceasing wonder, to the very end at Appomattox, to see how our lean, ill-equipped ranks would fight, all the harder, it seemed, as the men grew thinner and more ragged and hungry looking."

one

Sumter Light Guards, 4th Regiment Georgia Volunteer Infantry, C.S.A.

The American Civil War was fought by amateurs. In December, 1860, the Regular Army of the United States numbered only 16,367 officers and men. These, along with a few thousand men who had served and been discharged, constituted the professional corps of the Union and Confederate armies. They were a very small drop in the huge armies which would eventually draw in 2,500,000 Federals and about 1,000,000 Confederates. The men who pitched into each other with such awful effectiveness at First and Second Manassas, Wilson's Creek, Shiloh, Sharpsburg, Perryville, Murfreesboro, Fredericksburg, Chancellorsville, Vicksburg, Chickamauga, the fights about Richmond and the scores of other Civil War conflicts were nonprofessionals drawn from civilian life, given a little training in the fundamentals of soldiering, and thrown almost immediately into battle. They learned to fight by fighting.

The overwhelming majority of these amateur soldiers were volunteers. For while both sides resorted to conscription—the Confederacy on April 16, 1862, and the North on March 3, 1863—the principal benefits of the draft were to stimulate volunteering and to retain in the ranks soldiers who had enlisted for short terms of service. Both governments permitted draftees to hire substitutes, and the proxies seem to have outnumbered the conscripts. Professor Fred Shannon estimates that Northern draft laws brought into the service a total of 170,000 men of whom nearly 120,000 were substitutes. Reliable figures are not available for the Southern side, but substitutes probably numbered 50,000 to 100,000, and it is doubtful if Confederate draft laws yielded as many as 100,000 bona fide conscripts.

The overwhelming majority of Civil War soldiers were American-born whites, of an extraordinary diversity. It would be difficult to find a nineteenth century occupation or profession that was not represented in the Union or Confederate ranks. The occupational background of Northern soldiers was considerably more varied than that of Confederates. Examination of 123 Union rolls containing 14,399 names selected in such a way as to give a fair sampling reveals more than 300 vocations. Farmers constitute nearly half of the sample; other well represented groups in the order of their frequency are: common laborers, carpenters, shoemakers, clerks, blacksmiths, painters, soldiers, mechanics, sailors, machinists, masons, printers, teamsters, and teachers. The list contains a few strange entries such as "gentleman," "gambler," "loafer," and "Jack-of-all-traids."

The wide range of occupation that could be found in a single company is shown by the roll of Company C, Second Regiment, New York Heavy Artillery:

Farmer	37	Spinner	2	Gold Beater	1
Laborer	36	Peddler	2	Confectioner	1
Boatman	13	Drover	2	Shipwright	1
Soldier	12	Seaman	2	Teacher	1
Blacksmith	9	House Mover	2	Pressman	1
Carpenter	9	Tinsmith	2	Chemist	1
Teamster	8	Boilerman	2	Barkeeper	1
Clerk	7	Cooper	2	Telegrapher	1
Shoemaker	7	Plumber	2	Fireman	1
Tailor	6	Bookbinder	2	Miller	1
Machinist	5	Musician	2	Compositor	1
Mechanic	5	Car Man	1	Wheelright	1
Painter	5	Bleacher	1	Coachman	1
Baker	4	Speculator	1	Pianist	1
Bricklayer	4	Paper Hanger	1	Bookkeeper	1
Butcher	4	Miner	1	Engineer	1
Mason	4	Brass Filer	1	Sugar Boiler	1
Printer	3	Reporter	1	Wool Stapler	1
Sailor	3	Waiter	1	Student	1
Gardener	3	Storekeeper	1	Brakeman	1
Copper Worker	2	Optician	1		

The occupational diversity which characterized the Union forces gave them a resourcefulness which stood them in good stead in camp, on the march, and during battle. If a wagon, steamboat, or locomotive broke down, more than likely some soldiers could be found close at hand who knew how to make it go again. If a howitzer or a musket failed to function, a number of men were usually available who could restore it to working order. If a soldier dropped his watch or broke his violin, he usually did not have to go outside his regiment to get it fixed. When a Southern town was captured and the occupying forces wanted a newspaper, they called out printers from their own ranks to take over the abandoned press and issue a sheet of their own, as did the First Minnesota at Berryville, Virginia, the Thirty-third Illinois at Ironton, Missouri, the Twelfth Wisconsin at Humboldt, Tennessee, and the Eleventh Kansas at Canehill, Arkansas.

U. S. Grant recounts in his *Personal Memoirs* how General G. M. Dodge's command of about eight thousand men rebuilt the railroad from Decatur to Nashville, a distance of 102 miles, in forty days:

"Blacksmith shops with all the iron and steel found in them, were moved up to the line of the road. Axemen were put to work getting out timber for bridges and cutting fuel for locomotives when the road should be completed. Car builders were set to work repairing

Private Walter M. Parker, 1st Florida Cavalry, C.S.A.

6

the locomotives and cars. Thus every branch of railroad building . . . was all going on at once and without the aid of a mechanic or laborer except what the command furnished."

Owing largely to the South's concentration on agriculture and the relatively limited opportunity that it offered to mechanics and artisans, Confederate armies were more homogeneous than those of the North. Even so, occupations represented in Southern ranks were numerous and varied. A check of 107 company rolls containing 9,000 names, well distributed as to unit and locality, discloses 5,600 farmers, 474 students, 472 laborers, 321 clerks, 318 mechanics, 222 carpenters, 138 merchants, 116 blacksmiths, and smaller groups of sailors, doctors, painters, teachers, shoemakers, lawyers, overseers, printers, masons, tailors, millers, engineers, coopers, bakers, and other vocational groups. Confederate rosters, like those of the Federals, contain their share of oddities. One Southerner is listed as a rogue, another as a convict, and several as gentlemen.

The age patterns of the opposing armies were very much alike. In almost every regiment boys marched side by side with men old enough to be their grandfathers. A sample of 11,000 men taken from Confederate descriptive rolls turned up one soldier who was 13 when he enlisted, 3 who were 14, 31 who were 15, 200 who were 16, and 366 who were 17. Eighteen-year-olds, the largest of the age groups, numbered 971. About four-fifths of the total sample fell within the 18 to 29 bracket. Men in their thirties numbered 1,784, or about one-sixth of the total; and those in the forties were 418, or about 1 in 25. Eighty-six were 50 to 59; 12 were 60 to 69; one was 70; and one was 73.

A representative group of 14,330 soldiers selected from Federal rosters included 3 who were 12 when they entered the service, 12 who were 13, 4 who were 14, 5 who were 15, 62 who were 16, and 160 who were 17. As with the Confederates, the 18-year-olds, who aggregated 2,136, were the most numerous age group. Seven-tenths of the sample were 18 to 29 inclusive. Soldiers in their thirties totaled 2,448, or about one-sixth; and those in their forties numbered 1,007, or about one-fourteenth. Twenty-eight of the 14,330 were 50 to 59, 3 were 60, 1 was 62, and 1 was 65.

Most of the very young in both armies were drummer boys. But a few of them were full-fledged soldiers. Charles Carter Hay stated in 1901 that he joined an Alabama regiment in 1861 at eleven and that when he surrendered in 1865 he lacked a month of being fifteen. If his claim be true, he may well have been the youngest combat Confederate. The youngest Federals discovered in the sampling of descriptive rolls, as previously noted, were twelve. But official rosters are not always accurate guides. The very old and the very young frequently deceived the mustering officers who recorded their ages. Wilson Black whom the *Photographic History of the Civil War* represents as the "youngest wounded soldier reported" appears from his picture to be considerably less than twelve, but his age is not given. The boy soldiers on both sides were notable for the good humor, resilience, and fortitude which they displayed in camp and on the march. A number of them were cited in official reports for gallantry on the field of battle.

E. Pollard who joined the Fifth North Carolina Regiment in July, 1862, as a substitute, and whose age appears in the records as seventy-three, was probably the oldest Confederate. Pollard spent most of his service in the hospital, and when he was discharged after a few months the examining surgeon noted that he was "incapable of performing the duties of a soldier on account of Rheumatism and old age." The Federals recruited more old men than did the Confederates. One Union regiment, the Thirty-seventh Iowa, organ-

Federal Soldier from New York

Private John W. Branch,
12th Tennessee Infantry, C.S.A.

ized in 1862 for guard duty, had on its rolls 145 men who had passed their sixtieth birth-day. One of the Graybeards, as this regiment was called, was an eighty-year-old soldier named Curtis King, who served for four and a half months in 1862–1863 before being discharged for disability. King seems to hold indisputable claim to the title "oldest soldier of the Civil War."

Most of those who wore the blue and the gray were neither boys nor old men. Slightly less than three-fourths (72.9 per cent) of a sample of 25,000 men taken from Union and Confederate rosters came within the 18 to 29 age group. Half of the 25,000 were farmers. The typical Civil War soldier then was a farmer between 18 and 29.

Thousands of foreigners marched and fought with both the blue and the gray. Among the Confederates about one out of every twenty or twenty-five was of alien birth; and among the Federals about one out of every four or five. Germans and Irishmen were by far the largest of the foreign groups, and together they probably outnumbered all other non-American nationalities combined. Federal forces contained several divisions that were predominately German, and both sides had their "Irish Brigades" and Irish generals. Major General Patrick Cleburne, a native of the County of Cork, died leading a Confederate

Unidentified Confederate Soldier

Private Robert Patterson,
12th Tennessee Infantry, C.S.A.

charge at Franklin. During the fight at Ocean Pond another Irish Confederate, Brigadier General Joseph Finnegan, yelled to his aide who was also his son, "Go to the rear, Finnegan, me b'ye, go to the rear! Ye know ye are yer mither's darlin'!"

Scandinavians, who were not frequently encountered among wearers of the gray, comprised a majority of some of the Union regiments from the Northwest. Colonel Hans Heg's Fifteenth Wisconsin Regiment contained 128 men whose first name was Ole.

Another large element in the opposing armies were the Negroes. Among Confederates most of the blacks were laborers or menials. Many slaveowning Confederates took "body servants" to camp with them to cook their food, wash their clothes, clean their quarters, and relieve them of other "ungentlemanly" chores; in a few instances soldiers even delegated to their Negroes such onerous tasks as walking guard, while they themselves supervised the activity from a comfortable perch on some nearby stump. Most privates had to dispense with their colored helpers after a few months, but some of the officers retained their Negroes until the end. The depletion of the servant corps was offset by the bringing in of additional Negroes for use as army teamsters, road workers, and fortification laborers so that soldiers employed in these capacities might be available for combat. The number of Negroes who served in these auxiliary positions cannot be ascertained, but it ran to many thousands. General Nathan B. Forrest and Wade Hampton used their own slaves as wagoners for their commands.

On March 13, 1865, the Confederacy, after a long and bitter controversy, adopted a law authorizing the enlistment of 300,000 Negroes to serve as soldiers. A few colored companies were organized, and residents of Richmond in the last weeks of the war were treated to the spectacle of colored bondsmen marching down the street in shiny new uniforms. Little white boys who lined the sidewalks were said to have registered their contempt for the black soldiers by "pelting the fine uniforms with mud." The Confederacy collapsed before any of these troops could be committed to combat.

Body servants occasionally sneaked up to the front and took pot shots at the Federals, and persons possessed of enough Negro blood to merit classification by law as colored doubtless joined in the charges of Southern white regiments. But no evidence can be found of Negroes recognizable as such fighting as full-fledged Confederate soldiers.

Three Privates of the 3rd Georgia Infantry
Christopher C. Taylor, James D. Jackson, James H. Porter

On the Northern side, Federal authorities hesitated a long time before accepting Negroes as soldiers and then employed them only sparingly in combat. All told, about 200,000 Negroes donned the Federal uniform, and probably an equal number were connected with the Northern armies as cooks, wagoners, and laborers. One Union subaltern, just twenty-two, wrote proudly to his homefolk: "I have a little nigger to wait on me and am growing quite respectably corpulent in my old age. How much easier it is to have a little nig to take your extra steps for you than it is to do it all yourself." A Connecticut captain reported from Louisiana in 1862 that his regiment had no less than sixty "contrabands" * in its service.

The great majority of Negroes who wore the blue were former slaves, though a number of colored regiments, including the Fifty-fourth and Fifty-fifth Massachusetts, were composed largely of free men from the North. Many Negroes served as corporals and sergeants, but only a few were commissioned as officers. Until the summer of 1864 colored troops received only about half the pay given their white comrades, and when finally compensation was equalized the adjustment was not made retroactive.

The service of Negro soldiers was restricted largely to guard and labor duties. Protest against excessive use of them as "diggers and drudges" led the War Department in 1864 to issue a general order providing that the colored soldiers were henceforth to perform only their "fair share of fatigue duty." During the last two years of the war Negro troops participated in a number of battles, including Port Hudson (May 27, 1863), Milliken's Bend (June 7, 1863), Fort Wagner (July 18, 1863), Olustee (February 20, 1864), the Crater (July 30, 1864), and Nashville (December 15–16, 1864). The tendency of anti-Negro groups to belittle the colored soldiers and abolitionists to overpraise them makes it difficult for the historian to evaluate their combat performance. Some of them undoubtedly skulked and ran when the bullets began to whine about their heads; others displayed gallantry of the highest order. At Port Hudson a Negro sergeant died hugging the colors that had been entrusted to him when his regiment left New Orleans; on first receiving the emblem he had said, "Colonel, I will bring back these colors in honor or report to God the reason why." After Milliken's Bend, M. M. Miller, a white captain who had left Yale to command a Negro company, wrote to his aunt that he had "six broken bayonets to show how bravely my men fought." Negro troops could expect a special fury from their antagonists, for Confederates resented deeply the North's policy of arming freedmen. Thus, while Fort Pillow was not the massacre that Northern propagandists represented it, evidence gleaned from Southern sources leaves little doubt that in other engagements, if not at Fort Pillow, black Federals were shot down after they surrendered.

Literacy and intellectual interests of Civil War soldiers varied greatly. Extremes were represented by a highly cultured group at the top who carried Greek or Latin books in their haversacks and engaged in philosophic discussions about the campfire and a larger group at the opposite end of the scale who could not read at all and whose talk, heavily sprinkled with "hain'ts," "narys," "hits," and "have saws," rarely extended beyond such fundamentals as rations, women, officers, and home. Owing to the South's deficiencies in public educa-

---

* In May, 1861, several fugitive slaves from Hampton, Virginia, came into General Benjamin F. Butler's lines at Fort Monroe. Federal policy at that time required the return of runaway Negroes to their owners. On questioning the Negroes, Butler discovered that they had been employed in erecting Confederate defenses. He immediately declared them to be "contraband of war," subject to confiscation, and ordered them to be retained in the Federal camp. Thus originated the nickname of "contrabands" for fugitive slaves within Federal lines.

tion, illiteracy was greater among Confederates than among Federals. In some companies from the rural South half of the men could not sign the muster rolls. Such companies were exceptional, but so were those that did not have from one to a score who could not write their names. Sergeant Major John A. Cobb of the Sixteenth Georgia Regiment wrote to his uncle on September 8, 1861: "Paying off soldiers is a good deal like paying off negroes their cotton money and they are about as hard to understand what is coming to them. . . . About one-third of the men in the regiment cant write their names, so the Pay Roll has a good many X (his mark) on it and about one half of those that write them you cant read nor could they themselves." Of course, there were a few élite Confederate units such as the Richmond Howitzers, the First Maryland Infantry, Companies E and F of the First Virginia Infantry, and the Oglethorpe Light Infantry of Savannah in which the majority of the initial complement were men of education and culture.

On the Northern side the illiteracy rate was highest among Negro units recruited in the South, but the average Union regiment seems to have had no more than a half-dozen illiterates and many had none at all.

The thought patterns of Federals and Confederates were so diverse and complex as to make them difficult to isolate and define. In general they reflected the ideas and attitudes of the lower and middle classes from which nearly all of the common soldiers came. City-bred soldiers were inclined to classify themselves a few notches above their rural comrades, and country troops in turn berated urbanites as city slickers and parlor soldiers. Troops from the East were prone to consider themselves superior to those from the hinterland, and Westerners were just as quick to take a similar view of Easterners. Sectional bias was aided and abetted by interarmy jealousy. When Willis D. Maier, a Hoosier private in Rosecrans's Army of the Cumberland, heard of Meade's victory at Gettysburg he wrote: "it was time they were doing something. . . . We have fought the most stubborn Battles of this war but . . . our praise has gone to . . . the band box army on the Potomac, they needed it to keep up the spirit and we kept ours up by Victorious Battles." In 1864 a captain of Meade's army stated: "the Western rebels are not anything but an armed mob and not anything near so hard to whip as Lee's well disciplined soldiers." When troops from Burnside's command were sent to reinforce Grant in Mississippi in 1863, they taunted the Westerners with such questions as, "Who took Jackson for you?" and, "Who had to come away out here to take a one-horse town like Vicksburg?" Instead of being welcomed by their Western comrades, Eastern Federals who made the long trip to Chattanooga after Chickamauga were treated to such jeering salutations as "Bull Run," "All Quiet on the Potomac," and "Fall back on your straw and fresh butter."

Similarly Confederates of the Army of Tennessee disparaged Lee's soldiers as "Jeff Davis pets," while followers of "Marse Robert" belittled their Western counterparts as lazy, soft, and ineffectual. A Southerner who helped win the great victory at Chancellorsville wrote shortly afterward to his father in Alabama: "If the armys of the West were worth a goober we would soon have piece on our own terms."

As a general rule sectional antipathies found adequate release in taunting and jeering, but occasionally they erupted into violence. Henry P. Whipple, a Wisconsin private, wrote in his diary shortly after the arrival in Louisiana of some reinforcements from the East: "They and the Western boys fight every time we meet. I think either side would rather shoot at each other than the Johnnies."

12

Federal Soldier from Ohio

13

Private William A. Wyatt, 117th Illinois Infantry, U.S.A.

Benjamin F. Sawyer of the Twenty-fourth Alabama Regiment registered a sentiment popular among infantrymen of both armies when he stated that "every cavalryman ought to have a board tied on his back and the word 'thief' written on it so that honest men could know them when they came about." When a group of cavalrymen passed a column of infantrymen on the march, the foot soldiers would hurl at them such scornful comments as: "Better hurry, boys, or you'll miss your buttermilk!" "Why the haste, boys; is the enemy after you? Don't you worry, we'll protect you!" The riders usually paid no attention to the derision, but occasionally one of them would retort with such statements as, "Out of the way, mud-sloggers, and give the real fighters a chance"; and, "Watch out, webfoot or you'll get your paddlers smashed." Infantrymen of both armies passed on with approving chortles a statement attributed to some favorite among their generals: "I have yet to see on the battlefield a dead cavalryman with spurs on." There was, of course, a bit of envy concealed beneath the infantrymen's contemptuous remarks. This was plainly revealed in the advice sent by one veteran marcher to a younger brother about to enter the army: "Tell Him . . . by all means to Join the Cavalry—and bear in mind that a private in The Infantry is the worse place he can possibly be put in this war—so if he wants to have a good time Join the Cavalry."

14

The degree of antipathy held by Federals and Confederates toward each other varied considerably with individuals and circumstances. Some soldiers seem to have regarded their enemies with deep hatred from the beginning to the end of their service. Others entered the war with little or no hostile sentiment and were transformed into haters by their experiences. Others followed an opposite course, from initial hostility to friendliness toward their enemies. Still others alternated between hatred, indifference, and cor-

Private George W. Crane, 26th Illinois Infantry, U.S.A.

diality. Probably the great majority on both sides never felt any strong personal animus toward their foes as individuals. This impression is borne out by the ease and frequency with which the men of opposing armies got together to talk, to trade, to feast on wild berries ripening between the lines as they did at Vicksburg, to drink, to gamble, and even to swim and play. Fraternization was greatly facilitated by the fact that they spoke the same language and had similar backgrounds.

Consideration of the various attitudes and relationships gives rise to the question: What did these men believe they were fighting for? This is not an easy question to answer, for personal motivations are hard to establish and they differ with individuals. But letters and diaries leave the impression that the dominant incentive of most Confederates was to protect home and country from what they regarded as unwarranted invasion. As the average Southerner saw it, he and his comrades wanted only to follow in the paths of their fathers in matters of government, social institutions, and ways of earning a livelihood. He wanted to maintain the *status quo* and be left alone. But the North, motivated by greed, misled by wrong-thinking zealots and intoxicated by prosperity and power, seemed bent on upsetting the balance between state and national authority as laid down in the Constitution, relegating the South to a subordinate position, destroying the institution of slavery, and forcing upon the land of Dixie the horrible specter of social equality. When the South, for the protection of its ideas and institutions, exercised the constitutional right of secession, the North sent armies to compel its submission. The ordinary Confederate comprehended the constitutional issues only vaguely. But he had no difficulty realizing that his region and his family were imperiled by invasion, and he was firmly convinced that the aim of the invaders was to free the slaves. He was not primarily interested in slaves as property, for relatively few—certainly no more than one in five—soldiers owned slaves. But he had no qualms about the rightness of the institution and he was tremendously interested in slavery as an effective means of perpetuating white supremacy. The politicians, newspaper editors, and even the preachers told him that the overthrow of slavery would mean that his womenfolk would be insulted on the streets by Negroes and that emancipation would lead eventually to mongrelization; and he believed them. So he was fighting for slavery, not because of any pecuniary interest in it, but because of what it represented— along with states' rights, free trade, and the privilege to be let alone.

As for Northerners, the basic motivation of some was a desire to free the slaves, and there can be no doubt that many of those who took up arms for this cause derived from their convictions a strength which helped them to prevail over hardships, reverses, and perils of the most trying sort. The followers of Emerson, Garrison, Grimké, and Weld gave to the North some of its sturdiest and bravest soldiers. But the number of those who fought for emancipation was relatively small. Study of the letters and diaries of common soldiers indicates that no more than one in ten was seriously interested in releasing the Negroes from their bondage.

A far greater number fought to preserve the Union and, while most Federals—like most of the men who wore the gray—manifested little if any concern for ideological issues, there can be no doubt that "the Union" gave to the North its most effective rallying cry and its greatest and most enduring source of strength. Devotion to the Union was especially strong among Federals of foreign birth, many of whom had come to America to escape the division and strife that had torn their native countries. Hence they felt a peculiar responsibility for preventing a similar fate from overtaking the promised land of their adoption. In the letters of both the immigrant and native soldiers the phrase "fighting to maintain the best government on earth" is repeatedly encountered. This phrase doubtless had different meaning to those who used it. But to most if not all it must have represented a strong attachment to the nation which had been founded on the liberal ideals of the Revolutionary Fathers and which had become a symbol of hope for lovers of freedom and democracy throughout the world.

Unquestionably love of the Union was strong and deep among wearers of the blue. Thousands of them gave tangible evidence of their patriotism by re-enlisting in 1864 when they could have gone home with justification and honor. But they knew that their experience and hardihood were vital to the success of their cause, and at Spotsylvania, Cold Harbor, Kenesaw Mountain, Atlanta, Fisher's Hill, and Petersburg many of them gave their lives as indisputable testimonial to their undying devotion to the Union whose standards they had so proudly followed.

The spirit which motivated the soldiers of the North was vividly demonstrated by a conversation between a Union and a Confederate private as they lay wounded in a barn at Cedar Mountain on August 10, 1862. "For a while they eased their pain with banter and light talk. Then quiet fell, and presently the man who had lost a leg inquired calmly: 'Why did you come down here anyway, fighting us?' Equally without emotion but with much pride, the man in blue, whose arm was gone, replied: 'For the old flag.'"

Presentation of Colors to 1st Michigan Infantry, Cadillac Square, Detroit, Michigan, May 11, 1861,
Two Days Before Leaving for Washington

"Joining Up"

"The men whom we as Cavalry or Artillery dubbed 'flat feet' and 'dust beaters' and often ridiculed on the march."

two

Inspection of Regiment at Fort Wayne

two

The forty hours of shelling which led to the Federal evacuation of Fort Sumter on April 14, 1861, killed not a man; but it aroused both North and South to such a pitch that ordinary citizens seemed under a spell of camp-meeting hysteria. A citizen of Mansfield, Ohio, wrote to a friend on April 25, 1861: "Every boddy is running Crazy or mad, this County has already Started Eight Companies of Soldiers and as many more could be raised without any trouble . . . the old men who are too old to go . . . furnish the men with Horses free gratis, the Excitement runs so high that hundreds would give the last shirt to their backs." About the same time a resident of Albermarle County, Virginia, wrote to his governor: "All of us are . . . ripe and ready for the fight. . . . I shall be shoulder to shoulder with you whenever the fight comes off. I go for taking Boston & Cincinati. I go for wipeing them out." Another Virginian who had already sent five sons and a Negro servant to camp offered the governor the services of his "one single daughter"; and on May 10th a Georgia woman wrote: "We have formed a Female Company in Bascom for the purpose of learning to shoot. . . . The name of the company is the Bascom Home Guards."

A vivid glimpse of how people felt is afforded by the letter of a young Vermonter to a friend who had just entered the service. "I was glad to here that you was well," he wrote on June 9, 1861, "but still more so to here that you Enlisted to go and fight for your Country. Oh how I wish I could go. I cant hardly controll my self I here the solgers druming round. If you get your eye on old Jef Davis make a cathole threw him." A Georgian who was similarly stirred, later recalled: "The first time I heard Dixie I felt like I could take a cornstalk, get on the Mason and Dixon's line, and whip the whole Yankee nation."

In the emotionally surcharged weeks that followed Sumter's fall, the farms, factories,

22

countinghouses, railroad shops, lumber camps, crossroads stores, academies, colleges, and even theological schools showered a rain of manhood into streams that coursed through North and South, increasing in width and depth as they flowed, until finally they produced the tides which first surged into each other at Bull Run, Wilson's Creek, and Belmont and then subsided and were replenished by other outpourings from the same sources and with similar results.

But the initial mobilization was different in that it was so enthusiastic and spontaneous. It had a certain innocence, optimism, and urgency that were lacking in responses to subsequent calls for men. Many of the Southerners and Northerners who exchanged civilian clothes for uniforms after 1861, enlisted to forestall conscription or avoid public censure. Nearly all of those who flocked to the colors in the first few months of the war went because they could not endure the thought of staying at home; and their greatest fear was that peace would be made before they could get a taste of battle.

Indeed, the big problem in 1861 was to restrain the tide of volunteers so as to prevent the utter disruption of civilian activities and enable authorities to develop facilities for inducting, equipping, and training the recruits. Governor Dennison of Ohio on April 22, 1861, urged the national government to permit him to accept more than the thirteen regiments specified in Lincoln's call of April 15th. "Without seriously repressing the ardor of the people," he stated, "I can hardly stop short of twenty regiments." About the same time Governor Pettus of Mississippi wrote to Jefferson Davis: "All Mississippi is in a fever to get to the field"; and a little later Davis informed General Joseph E. Johnston: "From Mississippi I could get 20,000 men who impatiently wait for notice that they can be armed. In Georgia numerous tenders are made to serve for any time at any place and to these and other offers I am still constrained to answer, 'I have not arms to supply you.'"

Enlistment, in 1861 or later, followed a pattern that varied little in its essential features on either side. The first step was to sign a list circulated among prospective recruits by the individuals who expected to become the officers of the units. Sometimes mass meetings were arranged to expedite the process, though in the early days of the conflict this was not necessary. After signing their names on the roll, recruits usually had a few days of freedom, pending the filling up of the ranks of the company, which they devoted to arranging personal affairs and saying farewells. The visiting was fun, but taking leave of loved ones was a solemn occasion. Leander Stillwell, an Illinois soldier, described his experience thus:

Our parting was simple and unaffected, without any display of emotion by anybody. But mother's eyes looked unusually bright, and she didn't linger after she had said, "Good-bye Leander." As for my father,—he was an old North Carolinian, born and reared among the Cherokee Indians at the base of the Great Smoky Mountains, and with him, and all other men of his type, any yielding to "womanish" feelings was looked on as almost disgraceful. His farewell words were few, and concise, and spoken in his ordinary tone and manner, he then turned on his heel, and was gone.

Parents, as in all other wars in history, warned their departing sons against the evils of camp and gave them a few words of homely advice. William Andrew Fletcher recalled that when he left Beaumont to join the Fifth Texas Regiment his father said: "William I have long years since seen this had to come and it is a foolish undertaking, as there is no earthly show for Southern success as our ports will be blocked and the north will not only have the advantage of men and means, but the world to draw from. . . . I have opposed it, but as it is here, I will say that you are doing the only honorable thing and that is defending your country."

Farewells over, the recruits either entrained or marched to a nearby camp to complete the organization of their regiment and to begin the process of becoming soldiers. One of the first items on the agenda was a physical examination. This was frequently so perfunctory as to be undeserving of the name. A Sanitary Commission official, after an extensive survey of Union forces, wrote to Lincoln in July, 1862, "The careless and superficial medical inspection of recruits made at least 25 per cent of the volunteer army raised last year, not only utterly useless, but a positive encumbrance and embarrassment, filling our hospitals with invalids."

After certification of their physical fitness, the volunteers were formally mustered into service. Many of them were inducted twice, first as state troops and then after an interval of several days or several weeks, depending on the readiness of the central government to receive them, as Union or Confederate soldiers. Induction into the national service was an impressive ceremony. After forming by companies, officers and men were inspected by a mustering officer following which each of them was required to swear that he would

Company of Infantry on Parade near Harpers Ferry, West Virginia

Federal Regiment Formed in Square Against Cavalry

"I found that my brigade was almost alone, except Sykes' regulars, who had formed square against cavalry, and were coming back."—*Memoirs of General William T. Sherman*, account of the Battle of Bull Run.

"bear true allegiance" to the United or Confederate States and "serve them honestly and faithfully against all their enemies or opposers whatsoever, and observe and obey the orders of the President . . . and obey the orders of the officers appointed over me according to the rules and articles for the government of the armies. . . ." Then the articles of war, numbering 101, and having identical content in both North and South, except for the words United States and Confederate States, were read. One of the articles stated that "after a non-commissioned officer or soldier shall have been duly enlisted and sworn, he shall not be dismissed the service without a discharge in writing." The swearing-in ceremony was the point of no return. Sometimes a volunteer changed his mind at the last minute, refused to take the oath and went home. But the reaction of most was that revealed by Allen Kingsbury of Boston, when he wrote to his parents on May 23, 1861: "Yesterday afternoon we were all sworn into the United States service for three years, so I am one of Uncle Sam's men now."

Even before they were formally inducted the recruits had made awkward beginnings at drill, standing guard, and other fundamentals of camp routine. At some point along the way they took time out to elect officers, a costly concession made to volunteers by both Union and Confederacy. As a rule the men elected only their company officers, who in turn chose the majors, lieutenant colonels, and colonels of the regiment. But in some instances the men were allowed to elect every officer from corporal to colonel. Usually, though not always, the election of captains was a perfunctory approval of those who had taken the lead in raising the companies. In the instance of lieutenants, heated contests sometimes took place. Public speeches, private persuasion, and the dispensing of delicacies were standard features of elections, and some aspirants for office used liquor freely to promote their cause. The successful candidates nearly always treated the voters, and those who suffered defeat sometimes resigned and went home. A New York soldier wrote to his homefolk that after an election in his company the man chosen first lieutenant "made a very good speech and invited us to join with him in a social glass of Brandy & water. The Col. said that it was against the rules to allow any drinking, but as this was an especial occasion he would allow it. Our Captn and 2nd Lieut. made also some remarks, after which, and repeated cheers, we retired for the night."

A luxury available to soldiers in the Civil War was the new science of photography. One of the first things which nearly every recruit did after drawing his uniform and equipment was to pay a visit to a "daguerrian artist" or photographer to have his "likeness" taken. Frequently he was not content to face the photographer with the single weapon provided by the government, but arrayed himself with one or more pistols and a bowie knift to impress on his friends and relatives his power to slay his adversaries. De Le Rosen, who operated a gallery in Shreveport, Louisiana, and who professed to take pictures "upon Glass, Silver, Iron, Paper, Patent Leather, etc. in the highest style of art," in July, 1861, advertised "Ambrotypes Taken for $1—Satisfaction guaranteed in every case." But his rates appear to have been exceptionally low. Edwin H. Fay, a Louisiana soldier who had a daguerreotype taken at Corinth in May, 1862, wrote to his wife that it had cost him $8. "It is not like me . . . but it is the best I could do," he stated; "I think you will burn it when you see it, at least you ought to." Unfortunately the picture was lost in transit, and she never received it.

After a brief sojourn in encampments near their homes, the volunteers received orders to proceed to the combat zone, generally referred to as "the seat of war." Imminency of the departure sent a thrill of excitement through camp and community and set in motion a series of farewell activities. These usually included the presentation of a flag by some pretty woman. The presentation speeches, reported in detail by the local newspapers, were very much alike whether the scene was Maine, Minnesota, Alabama, or North Carolina. The talk made by Mrs. A. H. Seaman when she presented a banner to the Louisiana Guards at New Orleans in April, 1861, is a fair sample of phrase and sentiment. "Gentlemen of the Louisiana Guards," she stated,

it is fit that we to whom nature has refused the privilege of sharing your perils and laurels in the defense of our common country should testify our appreciation of the ennobling patriotism that rallies you around the Southern Confederate standard. . . . The love of our homes, duty, independence and liberty, all, all demand that we should proclaim to the men of the South that women, too, are ready to give up their comforts, part with their fathers, brothers and husbands, rather than submit to degrading, fanatical oppression. Imbued with this spirit we have worked with our own hands this flag, which you will accept as a token of our allegiance and devotion to the cause of Southern independence. We confide this banner to your keeping feeling that your stout hearts will never falter while it floats over your ranks. Remember that our dearest hopes are gathered round it; be mindful that it is but the emblem of a cause than which there is none holier and nobler, and that victory must reward your efforts, as justice and truth must at last prevail over treachery and fanaticism. In this struggle for independence, let it be your motto that "The South may be exterminated, but conquered—never!"

The response of the officer or color sergeant who received the flag was as fulsome and as stereotyped as the presentation speech. Usually it was sprinkled with such phrases as "We receive this emblem with high-beating hearts and throbbing pulses." "We register a soldier's vow that no stain shall ever be found on its sacred folds save the blood of those who fall in its defense." "These colors will be a constant reminder of our duty to our homes and our cause, and on the battlefield will inspire us to deeds of valor." "We will return them in honor or perish in defense of the nation for which they stand."

At the conclusion of the speeches a drill was held for the benefit of the visitors, after which soldiers and civilians gathered about picnic tables loaded with food and drink furnished by friends and relatives.

On the day of departure the community usually assembled at the railway station or some other place of rendezvous and listened to the farewell exhortation of a minister.

Camp, Las Moras near Fort Clark, Texas, March, 1861

"After the surrender of San Antonio by Gen. Twiggs, State troops were organized in order to take possession of forts occupied by the U.S. Army. This is a true picture of a portion of said State troops encamping on the Las Moras, near Ft. Clark, on their way to the upper posts (Hudson, Lancaster and Davis)."

Then, laden with gifts, the new soldiers took their leave amidst a chorus of "goodbyes" and "good lucks."

Nineteenth century notions of propriety tended to restrain any manifestations of emotion. This attitude is indicated in an incident reported by William H. Shaw in a letter to a friend, April 25, 1861: "Whilst one Company was on parade and first Starting one of the men whilst bidding his Wife good buy Whimpered a little and Showed Signs of back-out. his Wife told him If he was agoing to Cry about it to pull of[f] his Breeches and she would put them on and go in his place and he might go home and tend the Farm, this hapened in the presants of four or five hundred People." But sadness there was, and quiet shedding of tears, both in public and in private. "Those little words, good night Papa, have rung in my ears ever since the knight I left," wrote one Northerner shortly after leaving home. And another, a few days after reaching his destination, wrote apologetically to his mother: "I suppose you think hard of me for coming away in the manner that I did, but I knew that it would unman me to bid you good by so I took it on a rush."

The trip to the seat of war, made sometimes by boat and sometimes by train and occasionally both, was a boisterous experience. The majority of the soldiers were young; they rebounded quickly from the sadness of leaving their loved ones; they were happy to escape the restraints and boredom of their past existences; and they were thrilled by the prospect of new sights and experiences. They were certain also that the issue would be decided in one or two battles and that they would return home shortly as conquering heroes. Why should they not be jubilant?

Many of them helped their enthusiasm along with hearty swigs of liquor otherwise known as "Oh Be Joyful" or "How Come You So." "I have never seen in all my days so much whiskey," wrote a member of Wade Hampton's command a short time after arriving in Virginia. Among the imbibers were some who had never drunk before. After all, a man goes to war only once, and tomorrow would take care of itself.

A South Carolinian wrote after the war that "this trip from Columbia to Richmond . . . beat anything that I ever saw for non-discipline and insubordination in solders." If they rode in cattle cars on improvised benches as many did—though some of the first regiments sent to the front traveled in special passenger cars decked with flags and banners—they knocked out the sides of the cars with the butts of their guns for better ventilation and to see the sights. Those who rode on open flatcars did not have to worry about fresh air or visibility, and the same was true of those who crowded the roofs of coaches and boxcars; though they experienced considerable discomfort. A South Carolinian who made the long trip to Richmond on a flatcar wrote, after reaching his destination, "The smoke blowing in my face produced such a soreness in my eyes that I was almost blind when I got to Petersburg." Conviviality, congestion, and carelessness resulted in crippling and fatal falls on almost every trip of any considerable distance.

The attitudes and experiences of soldiers en route to war were vividly described in the letters that they wrote home.

On July 23, 1861, W. H. Darlington, a member of the First Regiment, Pennsylvania Reserves, wrote to his mother from Baltimore:

We marched out of Camp Curtin & down to the cars to the tune of Dixies' Land. Getting on the cars which were altogether open above the seats which were 2 inch planks place crosswise . . . we got under way at long last & passed through little York where some companies . . . behaved

Lieutenant Parker (Right) and Soldiers of 4th Michigan Infantry, U.S.A.

badly, taking liquor from the bar of the tavern without leave. . . . Among other articles stolen was an untapped keg of lager. . . . One of them beat the head in with the butt of his musket. The beer shot up into the air 15 feet like a fountain and fell foaming on every person & thing in the car. . . . It was amusing to see them all trying to get out of the way.

A Confederate, who happened to be of English birth, wrote of his trip from Mobile to Corinth in April, 1861:

We picked up, at different stations, company after company likewise bound to Corinth, and our train gradually lengthened to fifty cars. Another and another train being filled, we at length formed three long trains with six engines, puffing along at the rate of twenty miles an hour. Such noises as the men made are indescribable. Some of us were in passenger cars, but the greater number had to put up with baggage cars having temporary seats; and for want of sufficient ventilation, muskets were freely used in knocking out the panels to admit air. Some passed days and nights, riotously, on the roof, and beguiled the time with playing cards, or, having violins and banjos, with singing and dancing, scarce heeding the many bridges that jeopardized their heads, or the uneasy and dangerous rolling of overloaded and ill-constructed cars.

To many of the recruits the train ride to the front was a new and formidable experience. "I was wide awake the whole way; I was afraid we were off the track every time we crossed a switch or came to a river," wrote a young Wisconsin soldier. A tunnel was an especially notable experience. "The sudden transition from daylight to darkness, produced a novel sensation to me," wrote a Mississippi man in his diary. And an Ohio soldier whose narrative abilities were much better than his spelling described thus an eastward journey over the Baltimore and Ohio: "We past through some of the damdes plases ever saw by mortel eyes We run under some of the god dames hills it was dark as the low regions of hell We past through one tunel too miles long."

Arrival at the seat of war, whether it was Maryland, Virginia, Missouri, Kentucky, or Tennessee, usually meant a change in the character of soldiering. During the first weeks of service, while they were near their homes, discipline had been lax and duties relatively light. Soldiers frequently addressed their superiors by their first names or greeted them as "sarge" or "cap" or "mister." Leaves were not difficult to obtain, and officers and men spent a considerable portion of their time in nearby towns and cities.

But whether in camp or at the front the American volunteer of the sixties, as foreign observers were quick to notice, never became regimented and militarized as European soldiers were. The American common man was more independent, more of an individual as a civilian than his Old World counterpart. And in accordance with the rule that armies tend to reflect the character of the nations from which they come, Northerners and Southerners who went to war in the 1860's retained many of their civilian traits and habits throughout their military careers. Von Steuben observed when he undertook the training of Washington's army: "You say to your [European] soldier 'Do this,' and he doeth it; but I am obliged to say [to the colonial] 'This is the reason why you ought to do that,' and he does it." The quality noted by von Steuben in the Revolutionary troops was equally evident in their Civil War descendants, though perhaps more so among Confederates than

Camp of 2nd Connecticut Infantry, Washington, D.C., April, 1861

Soldiers of Company B, 9th Mississippi Infantry, C.S.A., at Pensacola, Florida, 1861. Left to Right: Jas. Peques, Kinloch Falconer, John Fennel, Jas. Cunningham, Thos. W. Falconer, Jas. Sims, John T. Smith

The regiment rendered conspicuous service at Shiloh, April 6-7, 1862. On April 7th, 1862, its commander, Lieutenant Colonel William A. Rankin, fell mortally wounded after having led his men fearlessly throughout the whole of the first and second days. The regiment was at the siege of Mumfordville and Woodsonville, the Stones River campaign, the Chickamauga campaign, and the Atlanta campaign.

among Federals. But among both, a certain irreverence for authority was discernible, and a tendency to figure things out for themselves. The average Confederate or Union soldier marched with a looseness which no amount of training could obliterate, and he fought the same way; but he was surprisingly effective. The army into which he was assimilated was not so disjointed as its parts.

Though Confederates and Federals always remained civilians in a degree, there was considerably less of the civilian in them at the end than at the beginning of their service. The time of greatest change usually was the period immediately following their arrival in the combat area. For there the certainty and imminency of fighting gave seriousness, purpose, and urgency to training. There the soldiers and their officers came under the jurisdiction of professionals like Joseph E. Johnston and George B. McClellan, Braxton Bragg and U. S. Grant, Robert E. Lee and C. F. Smith, leaders who knew that a transformation had to be wrought in the raw materials entrusted to them before battles could be won, who were willing to be strict and unpopular and who had the knowledge, skill, and prestige to do the job for which they were responsible. It took the professionals a while to make their influence felt, and some units were never converted into effective fighting organizations; but they were the exception rather than the rule. Evidence of a general tightening up is afforded by soldier letters and diaries. Many Federals and Con-

federates who during their first week in camp wrote of soldiering as if it were a lark, after they came under the aegis of the professionals began to complain of being treated like prisoners or Negroes. But as they became trained soldiers, inured to hardship, and especially as they learned in battle the value of discipline, most of them, despite their habitual growling, accepted and approved the new order.

After arrival in the combat area, the companies and regiments had to be welded into larger organizations. A platoon comprised two squads or sections, commanded by a lieutenant; two platoons comprised a company, commanded by a captain; ten companies a regiment, commanded by a colonel; two or more regiments a brigade, commanded by a brigadier general; two or more brigades a division, commanded by a major general; two or more divisions a corps, commanded by a lieutenant general on the Confederate side and a major general on the Union side; and two or more corps an army, commanded by a full general on the Confederate side and a major general on the Union side. Both North and South had separate infantry battalions, consisting usually of five to eight companies and commanded by lieutenant colonels; but except among the regulars on the Union side, battalions within infantry regiments were unusual. In the artillery, the battalion, consisting of four batteries each containing four to six guns, was a standard organization. The squadron (known also as the troop, and the equivalent, approximately, of the infantry company), consisting

Some of Sherman's Veterans, 21st Michigan Infantry, U.S.A.

The regiment fought in the battles of Perryville, Stones River, Chickamauga, and Chattanooga. It was on engineer duty in the last weeks of 1863 and in the early part of 1864 till June 11th, building hospitals, running mills, and so on. It was relieved from duty with the engineer brigade on September 20, 1864. It served under Sherman in the March to the Sea and in the campaign through the Carolinas January to April, 1865.

Soldiers of the 22nd New York State Militia in Camp at Harpers Ferry, West Virginia, 1862

of two or more platoons, was a distinctive feature of the cavalry organization. Combination of arms normally began with attachment of artillery (usually a battery) and cavalry to an infantry brigade. Engineer, signal, and other supporting elements were added on the corps or army level. The term "army group" does not appear in Civil War manuals, but Joseph E. Johnston, when he was placed over Pemberton and Bragg, and Grant and Sherman when they led the combined armies of the Cumberland, the Ohio, and the Tennessee were in effect army group commanders.

In 1863 the maximum authorized strength of the infantry regiment on the Union side was 39 officers and 986 enlisted men and on the Confederate side 49 officers and 1,340 enlisted men. But except during the early months of the war regiments rarely were at full strength. On the Union side, where as a general rule units were less depleted, the average strength of regiments in various engagements was: Shiloh, 560; Fair Oaks, 650; Chancellorsville, 530; Gettysburg, 375; Wilderness, 440; and Resaca, 305.

But the most important unit, and the one which formed the hard core of either army, was the infantry company. The "table of organization" for the Union company in 1863 was:

1 Captain	5 Sergeants
1 First Lieutenant	3 Corporals
1 Second Lieutenant	2 Musicians
	1 Wagoner

64 to 82 Privates

A Confederate company in 1863 included four officers—the fourth being known as a third or junior second lieutenant—5 sergeants, 5 corporals, and 64 to 125 privates.

Companies rarely approached full strength after the first few months of their existence. By 1864 many Confederate companies had dwindled to a score of men commanded by a lieutenant or a sergeant, and some Union companies were not much larger.

In terms of the whole period of the war and of men able to go into battle, it is reasonably accurate to think of Union and Confederate companies as groups composed of forty to sixty officers and men.

The smallness of the company was conducive to close association and intimate acquaintance. Indeed, the company was very much like a large family. The captain was the father who supervised daily routine; saw that his men were equipped, fed, clothed, and sheltered

Soldier Washing Clothes in Camp

Group of 4th Michigan Infantry, U.S.A.

A Group of Soldiers of Company G, 71st New York Infantry, U.S.A.

"The Seventy-first New York Infantry was organized as the second regiment of Sickles' brigade in June, 1861. The men left for Washington July 23rd. . . . They accompanied McClellan to the Peninsula, and served in all the great battles of the Army of the Potomac until they were mustered out at New York City, July 30, 1864. The regiment lost five officers and eighty-three enlisted men killed and mortally wounded, and two officers and seventy-three enlisted men by disease."

as well as circumstances permitted; heard their complaints; administered punishment for minor offenses; looked after their health; provided for their general welfare; and led them into battle. He knew every man by name and he was usually well acquainted with the home circumstances and even individual members of the soldier's family. His duties sometimes extended to mediating domestic squabbles, writing letters for those who could not write, superintending worship, burying the dead, and writing messages of condolence. A good captain usually meant a good company. The lieutenants, sergeants, and corporals were the captain's helpers; their position was comparable to that of the older children in a household. A key member was the first or orderly sergeant, who called the roll, kept the records, translated the captain's wishes into orders and, in general, acted as the medium of communication. As the company lived, marched, and fought together the members became so closely knit that they sometimes seemed to think and act as a single entity.

A Pennsylvania man put it well when he was fully embarked on the breaking-in process: "The first thing in the morning is drill, then drill, then drill, then drill again. Then drill, drill, drill, a little more drill. Then drill, and lastly drill. Between drills we drill and sometimes stop to eat a little and have roll call."

Since Hardee's manual of tactics, or a slight modification thereof, was used by infantrymen on both sides, training followed the same general pattern. At first recruits concentrated on exercises grouped in the manuals under the heading "school of the soldier," in which they learned such fundamentals as standing erect; facing left and right; saluting; marching forward, to the rear, by the flank and obliquely; shifting arms to the various positions; parrying and thrusting with the bayonet; and loading and firing their guns standing, kneeling, and lying down.

Loading "in nine times" as specified in the manuals was an intricate process; and usually a recruit was required to simulate the operation many times before being allowed to handle live cartridges and caps. The nine commands were executed thus:

1. *"Load!"* The soldier dropped the butt of the gun to the ground between his feet, grasped the barrel with his left hand and shifted his right hand to the cartridge box that hung on his belt.
2. *"Handle*—Cartridge!" The soldier seized the paper cartridge with his thumb and two fingers and placed the end containing the powder between his teeth.
3. *"Tear*—Cartridge!" The soldier bit off the end of the paper and moved the cartridge to the muzzle of the gun.
4. *"Charge*—Cartridge!" The soldier emptied the powder into the barrel, tore the paper from the bullet, pressed the bullet, base down, into the muzzle with his right thumb and seized the head of the ramrod fastened beneath the barrel.
5. *"Draw*—Rammer!" The soldier removed the rammer and placed its head against the bullet in the muzzle.
6. *"Ram*—Cartridge!" The soldier pressed the ball all the way down the barrel.
7. *"Return*—Rammer!" The soldier replaced the rammer beneath the barrel.
8. *"Prime!"* The soldier raised the gun, sloped it in his left hand across his body, brought the hammer to half-cock with his right thumb, removed a cap from the pouch on his belt, and placed the cap on the nipple.
9. *"Shoulder*—Arms!" The soldier shifted the gun to the carry position on his right shoulder.

After the loading was thus completed, firing was accomplished by a series of motions

Group of 4th Michigan Infantry, U.S.A.

Sergeant Edward Bussell, 22nd New York State Militia

executed at the commands, *Ready, Aim, Fire*. Despite the complexity of the procedure, a veteran infantryman could load and fire his rifle twice a minute from a standing position. Loading the long-barreled weapons from the prone position was a difficult task that required rolling over to insert the charge and ram it home; but soldiers mastered the technique.

Training in the 1860's, as today, was progressive. As Confederates and Federals acquired proficiency in handling their weapons and functioning as squads, they were introduced to "the school of the company." At this stage they learned to shift back and forth from column of fours—the usual, four-abreast, marching formation—to the two closely spaced ranks which constituted the line of battle. Drill-book instructions for these and other maneuvers were exceedingly involved, and sometimes officers had as much difficulty giving the proper commands as the men had in executing them. One day Captain Candler, a Georgian who had left his plantation to command his friends and neighbors of the Banks County Guards, decided to march his company from their camp to a large drill ground nearby. As the men proceeded down the road, led by the captain who was walking backward to keep his eye on the column, they approached an open gate. The captain could not think of the proper command, "By the right flank, file left," to get them through and they were about to press him into the fence. In his desperation he yelled out the order: "Gentlemen of the Banks County Guards! Will you please halt?" They stopped in the nick of time. He then

40

Gilbert Marbury, Drummer Boy (Age 17), 22nd New York State Militia

said: "Gentlemen, we will now take a recess of ten minutes. Break ranks! and when you fall in will you please re-form on the other side of the fence." Captain Candler later became Governor of Georgia.

Training at the company level was followed by "the school of the regiment" classified in the drill book as "school of the battalion." At this stage companies learned to maneuver as parts of the regiment. The next step was from regimental to brigade and division training. But training beyond the regimental level seems to have been exceedingly limited.

The procedure outlined above applied specifically to infantrymen, who constituted the bulk of both armies. But other branches followed a comparable routine. A vivid glimpse of the way in which artillerymen acquired proficiency is afforded by the following excerpt of a letter written by William M. Dame of the Richmond Howitzers to his mother:

The company has four guns; & it is divided into four detachments, giving one gun to each detachment; there are about 20 men in each detach[ment] & they are commanded by a sergeant & a corporal. . . . Each detachment is to see that their gun is kept in order, i.e., harness in good fix, gun clean, wheels well greased &c, &c. Whenever any of these things have to be done, the detachment is called out & the work done. Of these we are in the fourth detachment at present. I will explain our duties about the gun. In loading the piece, every man has a separate duty to perform. One has to take the ammunition out of the am'n chest, another has to carry it to the gun, another put it in, another ram it down &c. To do this without confusion the men have each a number. . . . No's 1, 2, 3, 4 & 5, the gunners, attend particularly to the piece; No. 6 takes out the ammunition & hands it to No. 7 & he to No. 8, he to 10 & he to No. 5 who carries it to the gun & hands it to No. 2 who puts it in the cannon & No. 1 rams it down. No. 3 pricks the cartridge with a little wire he has & No. 4 fires off the gun. Now in drilling the men take turns at the different numbers as in battle any one may be called on to take any No., but in battle the oldest cannoneers take the post of 1, 2, 3, 4, 5, as they are the most responsible & they are supposed to be more steady & cool in time of battle.

In the Civil War infantry training was only occasionally given the realism judged necessary by modern standards. Skirmish drill on the company and regimental level seems rarely to have been enlivened by the firing of blank cartridges. Target practice with live ammunition appears to have been limited largely to small groups going out with their officers or on their own and trying out their weapons on fence rails, saplings, or small game. When on rare occasions a brigade or division commander brought his infantry, artillery, and cavalry together and let them pitch into each other in simulated combat with blank ammunition, they made the hills and valleys resound with shouts of joy and excitement. After one of these exercises a Yank wrote his homefolk: "The Cavalry charged down on us and for the first time I saw something that looked like fighting. The artillery blazed away, and we had a regular sham battle. It was a beautiful sight and . . . we began to think we can whip twice our weight in Rebels."

Still another part of the breaking-in process was getting accustomed to the regimental day. Life in camp was regulated by drum or bugle calls, and these normally ran to about a dozen a day. The first was reveille, sounded at dawn or thereabouts, to rouse the men from their slumber and summon them to roll call. After lining up and responding to their names, they might be put through a brief and rapid drill; but usually they were left on their own until the second call about thirty minutes later hailed them to breakfast. The third signal shortly afterward sent the ailing to the regimental surgeon and the well to such fatigue duties as cleaning quarters, policing company grounds, and cutting wood.

At guard mounting, sounded about eight o'clock, the first sergeant of each company called out and inspected his detail for the next twenty-four-hour stint, and marched them to the regimental parade ground. There, to the accompaniment of music provided by the regimental band, the guards were formed into line, inspected by the adjutant, and sent to their respective posts. The next signal was for drill, which frequently lasted until the call, sometimes known as "roast beef," announced the time for lunch. After a brief interval of free time came another call for drill, which normally lasted from one to two hours. Drill over, the men returned to their quarters, brushed uniforms, polished buttons and buckles, and cleaned their weapons in anticipation of the call to retreat which consisted of roll call, inspection, and dress parade. Both officers and men took great pride in the dress parade, held sometimes by regiment and sometimes by brigade, and always to the accompaniment of music.

The call to supper was sounded shortly after retreat. Then came another period of free time, after which tattoo brought companies back into line to answer roll. Upon dismissal the men returned to their quarters. The day was officially concluded by the sounding of taps which signaled the extinguishing of lights and the cessation of noise.

This was typical routine for an infantry regiment during a period of quiet. Practices varied, of course, in different commands and with changing circumstances. Sunday routine was different from that of any other day. The big event of the Sabbath was a general

Camp of the 3rd Kentucky Infantry, C.S.A., near Corinth, Mississippi

Winter Quarters at Centreville, Virginia, Abandoned by the Confederate Army, 1862

inspection of personnel, equipment, quarters, grounds, kitchens, hospitals, and other facilities. Preliminary checks were made by the units' own officers. But the climax was inspection of the regiment or its equivalent in formation—Company A on the right, B on the left, and the others in between—by an outsider, usually the brigade commander or one of his staff. The inspector marched up and down the open ranks scrutinizing uniforms and arms, but he also poked into the knapsacks which the men had unslung, opened, and laid on the ground for his examination. Detection of the smallest particle of dirt or the slightest deviation from uniform regulations was almost certain to bring sharp reproof from the inspector and a tongue lashing from the captain after return to quarters.

This inspection and the preparations that it required consumed most of the morning. "Knapsack drill," as the Confederates and Federals called the Sunday exercise, was an exhausting experience, and soldiers of the sixties regarded it with dread. But like the other aspects of the regimentation of which it was a part, it helped mold undisciplined individuals into smoothly functioning organizations.

One important aspect of soldiering to which most Union and Confederate men were not introduced until after they left their home communities was payday. At the beginning of the war the pay scale in both armies was $11 a month for infantry and artillery privates and $12 for cavalry. Early in the conflict the pay of Union privates in all three branches

44

was raised to $13 a month and on May 1, 1864, to $16. Confederates received no increase until June 9, 1864, when the pay of all enlisted men was boosted $7 a month, making the pay of infantry and artillery privates $18 and that of cavalry $19. But at the time this increase was voted, the Confederate paper dollars in which payment was made were worth in gold only about five cents, and at a city market a month's pay would buy only two pounds of sugar or two large heads of cabbage, or a peck of meal or two pounds of bacon. Flour was $275 a barrel, shoes $125 a pair, and men's pants $125.

Soldiers were supposed to receive their pay every two months, but Union troops often had to wait three to six months, and Confederates much longer, before receiving their money. After a round of inspections in the District of West Louisiana in November, 1864, a Confederate officer reported that many of the regiments had not been paid for twelve months; and one of Hood's soldiers wrote from near Atlanta in August, 1864, that he and his comrades had gone without pay for thirteen months.

Troops were mustered for pay by an inspector general or some other officer specially designated for the purpose. At the muster, which normally included a review and inspection, the visiting officer called the names on the company roll. When a soldier heard his name he answered, "Here," brought his gun quickly to the carry position and then dropped the butt to the ground and held it in the position of "order arms." After every man in the company had been accounted for, the mustering officer forwarded a copy of the muster roll to the adjutant general and this became the basis for the pay which subsequently was transmitted by paymasters to unit commanders for distribution to their men. The money was received with enthusiasm regardless of when it came or in what amounts. One Federal humorously observed that "a paymaster's arrival will produce more joy in camp than is said to have been produced in heaven over the one sinner that repenteth." Northern soldiers could send a portion of their wages home under a voluntary system of allotment initiated in 1861, but no such arrangement seems to have been available to Confederates.

Company Street

Rations

three

Pork, Hardtack, Sugar, and Coffee for the Army, Commissary Depot, Cedar Level, Virginia, 1864

three

"I am so hungry I could eat a rider off his horse and snap at the stirrups," wrote a Minnesota soldier from Chattanooga in August, 1864. And a famished Texan, while stationed in the same locality the previous year, remarked that if he was ever so fortunate as to get back to his father's house he intended "to take a hundred biscuit and two large hams, call it three days rations, then go down on Goat Island, and eat it all at ONE MEAL."

The hunger of which these men complained was not due to any lack of generosity on the part of their governments. The ration officially prescribed for both sides at the beginning of the war was that of the United States *Army Regulations* of 1857. This provided a daily allowance for each soldier of

twelve ounces of pork or bacon, or, one pound and four ounces of salt or fresh beef; one pound and six ounces of soft bread or flour, or, one pound of hard bread, or, one pound and four ounces of corn meal; and to every one hundred rations, fifteen pounds of beans or peas, and ten pounds of rice or hominy; ten pounds of green coffee, or, eight pounds of roasted (or roasted and ground) coffee, or, one pound and eight ounces of tea; fifteen pounds of sugar; four quarts of vinegar; . . . three pounds and twelve ounces of salt; four ounces of pepper; thirty pounds of potatoes, when practicable, and one quart of molasses.

In terms of the fare authorized in European countries, this was an abundant allowance. It was about one-fifth more than that of the British, nearly twice that of the French, and compared even more favorably with that of the Prussians, Austrians, and Russians. The Union Government, not content with the relative bountifulness of the old order, in August, 1861, increased the bread ration by four ounces and provided a greater variety of other items. This augmented ration, accurately described by Surgeon General William A. Ham-

50

mond as the best in the world, remained in use until June 20, 1864, when it was replaced by the original allowance. Nearly three years' experience had shown that the enlarged issue encouraged wastefulness on the part of the soldiers, increased the cost of sustaining the armies, and intensified problems of logistics.

The Confederacy was not able to retain the 1857 ration, much less increase it. Early in the conflict field commanders had to order reductions in the meat issue and to make various substitutions for other items, such as rye for coffee and molasses for sugar; and in the spring of 1862 the Confederate War Department was compelled to cut the daily meat ration by four ounces.

In actual fact the rations specified in regulations and the fare actually served in camp varied widely in both armies. As a general rule, Northerners enjoyed a considerably greater abundance and variety of food than did Southerners, and the latter were acutely aware of the disparity. Near the end of the war, according to a story that had wide currency among Southerners, a bedraggled, hungry, and sickly Confederate spied a mounted Federal who was splendidly attired and obviously well nourished. "Oh, my, oh, my! you look like you wuz sich a happy man!" said the Southerner. "You got on sich a nice new-niform, you got sich nice boots on, you ridin' sich a nice hoss, an' you look like yer bowels wuz so reglar."

The quantity and quality of the rations varied greatly with changing circumstances. During the long intervals between campaigns when the armies were stationary, rations were relatively plentiful. Conversely, when the armies were on the move or engaged in battle, haversacks and stomachs often were empty.

The facilities for procurement, storage, and distribution were a basic factor in rationing the armies. Both North and South produced more than enough meat, wheat, corn, potatoes, beans, peas, and other essentials to feed the civilians and soldiers. The North, owing to the excellence of its rail and steamship lines, and the expertness with which they were utilized, was able as a general rule to transport foodstuffs to the places needed, and to preserve them until they were dispensed to the consumers. The Confederacy, on the other hand, was so handicapped by dearth of rail lines—at the beginning of the war, the eleven seceding states had only 9,000 miles of railroad as against 21,000 in the Northern states—and other shipping facilities, and made such poor use of what it had, that it was not able to transport in ample quantities provisions grown at home to armies in the field. The South did not have enough salt to preserve its meat. Moreover, inflation and the fear of impressment caused planters and farmers to hoard their surpluses. Added to all these difficulties was a shocking amount of ineptitude and mismanagement in supply administration, from the highest to the lowest levels and including the Commissary General Lucius B. Northrop. Thus, despite the production of abundant crops in uninvaded areas every year of the war, Confederate soldiers were often hungry. In mid-February, 1865, Governor Zebulon Vance of North Carolina publicly declared that "hundreds of thousands of bushels of Grain now rot at the various depots of the South for want of transportation," and a month before Lee's surrender a commissary official in Richmond stated that 12,500,000 bread rations and 11,500,000 meat rations could be obtained in North Carolina and Virginia for army use if the government had means to buy and transport them.

But lean seasons were by no means peculiar to the Confederacy. Numerous instances of deprivation occurred in 1862 among Northern soldiers stationed in Missouri and Arkansas and among those serving with Buell in Kentucky and Frémont in Virginia. Yet the commands involved were small and the periods of want usually brief. The first widespread food shortage on the Northern side occurred in the Army of the Potomac in the war's second winter when Burnside was "stuck in the mud" opposite Fredericksburg. During this period soldiers frequented the slaughter pens looking for heads, tails, and feet of steers to assuage their hunger. Beef bones discarded by one Federal were eagerly retrieved by another and passed from man to man until every particle of flesh had been removed. "I live on faith and sour wheat bread," wrote one famished Federal to his homefolk, and another informed his sweetheart that "we have but two beans to a pint of water."

Some of Grant's troops were on severely reduced rations during the campaign in north Mississippi late in 1862 and the advance on Vicksburg the next spring. But the worst famine on the Union side was that experienced by the soldiers who participated in the Chattanooga and Knoxville campaigns of late 1863. When Bragg bottled up the Army of the Cumberland after Chickamauga, hungry Federals would follow commissary wagons and raid the

Hardtack and Field Eating Utensils Used by a Union Soldier

Officers' Mess, Company F, 93rd New York Infantry, U.S.A. Headquarters, Army of the Potomac, August, 1863

horse troughs to get a few grains of corn to supplement their meager fare. Private Willis D. Maier, a young man from Indiana who usually was buoyant and gay, wrote morosely to a friend on October 22nd from Chattanooga that for the past month he and his comrades had been living on "two meals per day and one cracker for each meal. I was nearer starved here than ever." Grant's opening of the Tennessee River a short time later brought relief to the troops about Chattanooga, but soldiers who in December marched from that city to Knoxville and back with only three days' rations suffered terrible hunger.

The first severe pinch on the Confederate side seems to have occurred at Fort Donelson in February, 1862, just before the surrender; but only a few weeks later D. H. Hill's division and other units engaged in the withdrawal up the Virginia peninsula lived for three days on parched corn. Lee's march into Maryland and Bragg's invasion of Kentucky were occasions of considerable want, and the same was true of the Gettysburg and Chattanooga campaigns of the next year. But the hunger suffered on these expeditions was mild in

53

comparison to that endured by the Confederates besieged at Vicksburg and Port Hudson. During the month and a half that they were sealed within their fastnesses the beleaguered men resorted to all sorts of expedients to stretch their ever dwindling fare. They ground field peas and rice to obtain "flour"; stewed green berries, half-grown peaches, roots, leaf buds, grass, and weeds to produce unpalatable broth; and at the very last they ate dogs, rats, and mules.

In 1864 Confederates who followed Early up and down the Shenandoah Valley and those who marched with Hood to Nashville and back sometimes had to subsist for two or three days on a slice or two of raw bacon, a handful of peanuts ("goober peas") or a few kernels of parched corn.

During the winter of 1863–1864, while his army was stationed near Orange Court House, General Robert E. Lee received in the mail a package containing a small piece of salt pork sandwiched between two oak chips. The accompanying message was not signed, but the sender indicated that he was a private and a gentleman and that since this was his daily meat ration he had been forced to steal to appease his gnawing hunger. However, the greatest misery experienced by the Army of Northern Virginia came during the retreat from Petersburg to Appomattox, when the troops were separated from the wagon trains and opportunities for foraging were virtually non-existent. A participant in this movement wrote that "two-day fasts were not uncommon," and that an artillery battalion subsisted for a week on corn drawn for the battery horses and raw bacon captured from the Federals. When, after the surrender, Grant ordered rations issued to the starving Confederates they had a feast comparable to that enjoyed under similar circumstances by Pemberton's men at Vicksburg.

The staples on both sides were meat and bread. Meat was either pork or beef—fresh, cured, or pickled. Fresh meat often was rancid, and pickled beef, which soldiers usually referred to as "salt horse," sometimes was putrid and nearly always so briny as to make it unpalatable. Pork, commonly known as "sowbelly"—one Federal with a bent for detail noted that it was served "with the tits on"—frequently was tainted or infested by maggots.

The poor quality of the rations on both sides inspired some eloquent denunciation. One Confederate wrote that commissaries at slaughtering time drove the beeves to a pole lying on the ground and that those unable to step over it were killed for the meat issue. Private William R. Stillwell of Georgia wrote that the bacon issued to his regiment was covered with "hare [sic], skin and dust and so rank that it can hardly be eat." Adrian Carruth of Mississippi declared that the beef drawn by his company was so rotten that "the buzzards would not eat it."

The comments of Federals were no less caustic. Elisha Stockwell of the Fourteenth Wisconsin Regiment wrote that beef drawn by his company during the Atlanta campaign "was so poor that there wouldn't be a bead of grease on a whole kettle after it was boiled." Joseph H. Diltz of Illinois wrote from Tennessee that the beef was so inferior "that one can throw a piece up against a tree and it will just stick there and quiver and twitch for all the world like one of those blue bellied lizards at home will do when you knock them off a fence rail." An Ohioan informed his homefolk that he had recently drawn meat "so damd full of skippers that it could move alone," and another Federal wrote: "Yesterday morning was the first time we had to carry our meat for the maggots always carried it till then. We had to have an extra gard to keep them from packing it clear off."

Of course, much of this disparagement was exaggerated, for soldiers will criticize their

54

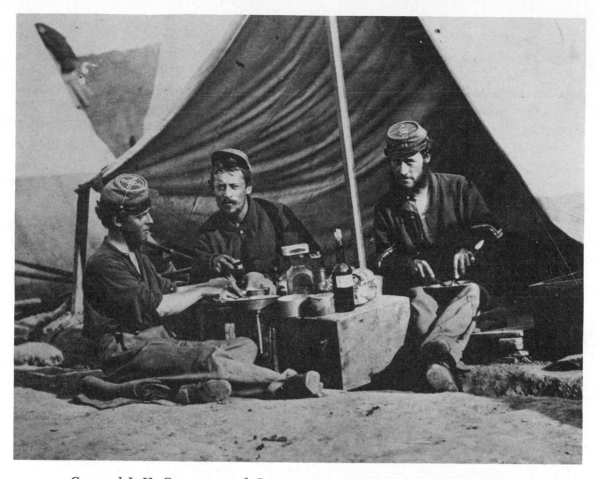

Corporal J. H. Carpenter and Group at Mess, 22nd New York State Militia

food whatever its quality, as a diversion and a release from their pent-up annoyance with discipline. Yet with due allowance for exaggeration, the meat issued to the soldiers left much to be desired.

The bread most commonly served to Confederates was cornbread, though frequently they drew loaves of flour bread and occasionally hardtack. When left to their own resources they often converted the flour issue into hoecakes or biscuits. Though normally fond of cornbread, the frequency with which it was served and the poor quality of the meal from which it was made caused the soldiers to become very tired of it. Johnny C. Murray, who wrote to a friend near the end of the war "that every morsel we have ate for the past week has been *corn bread*," registered a sentiment popular among Confederates when he concluded: "If any person offers me corn-bread after this war comes to a close, I shall *probably* tell him to—go to hell."

Union soldiers rarely ate cornbread, but when circumstances permitted, and when they had commanders such as Hooker who were keenly aware of the close relationship between rations and morale, they enjoyed the luxury of soft flour bread freshly baked in field ovens. But the bread ration with which they became most familiar was hardtack, also known as seabiscuit. Hardtack was a rectangular cracker 3½ inches wide, 2⅞ inches high, ⅜ of an inch thick and weighing about 1½ ounces. It came packed in barrels or wooden boxes, and a common mode of issuance was for the orderly sergeant to remove the lid and call out to the company, "Come and get your crackers," and permit the men to take as many as they wished. When doled out individually the day's issue per man was normally nine to twelve crackers, but during periods of scarcity the number might be reduced to three or four. The packages sometimes were marked with the letters "B. C.," which possibly stood for Brigade Commissary, but soldiers were positive that the stamp meant "Before Christ."

Some Yanks admittedly developed a fondness for hardtack, but they were very few. The crackers must have been hard. One soldier complained that his teeth were sore for days after he first ate them. Another declared that they "would make good brest works." A third avowed that he could not break them "without getting a pry on something," and

Killing the Bullocks

Commissary Department, Headquarters, Army of the Potomac, April, 1864

various others told of beating them with musket butts or soaking them for several hours in warm water to make them edible.

The crackers were often stale and moldy. The frequency with which they were infested by worms caused them to be dubbed "worm castles." One Union soldier counted thirty-two maggots in one cracker; another declared that "all the fresh meat we had came in the hard bread . . . and I, preferring my game cooked, used to toast my biscuit"; and a third complained that "the hard bread is all worms and the meat stinks like hell."

White beans, known as "army beans" were a frequent item of issue in Northern camps. Southern counterparts were field peas, sometimes of the black-eyed variety but more commonly the speckled "whip-poor-wills," which General Lee is said to have pronounced "the Confederacy's best friend." The peas were usually seasoned with bacon and boiled. Union troops normally parboiled and baked their beans, or used them as a principal ingredient in soup. For baking, the beans were frequently put in a pot, along with a hunk of meat, and the pot was buried from twelve to twenty-four hours in a hole lined with hot coals. When the lid was finally removed, the savory aroma summoned hungry men to a meal which they ate with great relish—especially if they were from New England.

Rice and potatoes were served in both armies as circumstances permitted. Sweet potatoes frequently were a part of Southern fare, and some Northern soldiers acquired a taste for them. Corn on the cob—known in the South as "roas'n' ears"—plucked from the growing stalks and boiled in pots or roasted in the shucks beneath a pile of hot ashes, had a high rating among soldiers of both sides. Molasses, served over "slap-jacks" or cornbread, was a common item in Confederate fare but was rarely issued to Federals.

Coffee was considered indispensable by Northern soldiers, and most of them consumed it in quantities which at home they would have regarded as grossly excessive. They liked it prepared according to specifications laid down by one of Sherman's veterans: "Black as the face of a plantation negro, 'strong enough to float an iron wedge,' and innocent of lacteal adulteration." Served thus, according to this veteran, "it gave strength to the weary and heavy laden and courage to the despondent and sick at heart." The blockade made coffee a very precious commodity in the South and compelled both civilians and soldiers to partake of poor substitutes brewed from parched peanuts, potatoes, peas, corn, and rye. "How much I miss the good coffee I used to get at home," wrote an ailing Texan in July, 1862; "I would cheerfully pay one dollar for as much as I could drink." But coffee was not to be had except at exorbitant blockade prices and sometimes it was not obtainable at all.

Federal commissaries sometimes dispensed a Civil War version of instant coffee known as "extract of coffee" or "essence of coffee," but this was not well received by the soldiers. Other newfangled foods known to Northerners were "desiccated vegetables"—which soldiers quickly perverted to "desecrated vegetables"—and "pulverized potatoes." Concerning the latter an Illinois veteran wrote: "It consisted of Irish potatoes cut up fine and thoroughly dried. In appearance it much resembled the modern preparation called 'grape nuts.' We would mix it in water, grease and salt, and make it up into little cakes, which we would fry and they were first rate." Another Northerner who rendered a less favorable judgment stated that the concentrate "does not taste much like potatoes."

Desiccated vegetables, as one soldier recalled them after the war, were a mixture "of all sorts of vegetables pressed into small bales in a solid mass, and as dry as threshed straw. The conglomeration contained turnip-tops, cabbage leaves, string-beans (pod and all) onion blades and possibly some of every other kind of vegetables. . . . In the process of cooking it would swell up prodigiously. . . . The Germans in the regiment would make big dishes of soup out of this 'baled hay,' as we called it, and they liked it, but the native Americans after one trial, wouldn't touch it." Another veteran, who remembered the compressed vegetables as "cakes about 10 by 12 inches square and about one inch in thickness," stated that they made a "first class" soup. He told of a comrade who made the mistake of eating one of the cakes raw and then after a while "lay on the ground, moaning, rolling and tossing," in great agony. "We thought he was going to die," he added; "his stomach looked as if he had a base drum in it, but after quite a siege he got relief."

Concentrated foods, with few exceptions, were spurned by Federals and not available to Confederates. Dearth of fresh vegetables was, in soldier opinion, at least, the most grievous deficiency in the army ration. "I am nearly perished for vegetables," wrote an Alabamian from near Atlanta in June, 1864, and he expressed a complaint frequently heard in both armies. One of the consequences of the shortage was a high rate of scurvy. The incidence of this malady was especially great among Confederates despite the efforts of commanding officers and surgeons to forestall it by sending soldiers to the fields in search of wild onions, water cress, dandelion, artichoke, and poke shoots.

Army regulations of both sides authorized commanding officers, at their discretion, to issue a gill (one-quarter of a pint) of whisky per day to each of their men during periods

Federal Soldiers Filling Canteens, Fredericksburg, Virginia, May, 1864

Soldiers are waiting their turn to dip their canteens in a covered well or cistern. The three men sitting on horses are colored personal servants; it was common for them to wear items of soldier apparel. Servants could be hired for a nominal sum—a couple of dollars a week—from among the fugitive slaves. More than one Northern enlisted man wrote home, after he had been in the South for a while, "I have got me a (little) nigger to do my cooking, wash my clothes and look after my horse."

of "*excessive* fatigue or *severe* exposure." Most Union commanders took advantage of this provision; but Confederate leaders, owing to the scarcity of liquor and a widespread tendency of Southerners to regard drinking as sinful, rarely dispensed whisky to their men.

Soldiers were not solely dependent on their governments for subsistence. Commissary issues were often supplemented by food sent from home. The volume and variety of edibles that poured into camps throughout the conflict from Northern and Southern communities was tremendous. Boxes packed with cakes, pies, bread, butter, cheese, pickles, ham, honey, preserves, potatoes, squash, brandy and wine were transported over great distances and to the remotest places by common carriers, friends, and relatives. The lengths to which personal emissaries sometimes would go to satisfy their friends is revealed by the message of a Virginian to his parents: "I got my pants and drawers safe & ten chickens. Mr. Simmons said a great many of them died he started with some 300 from home and lost some 25 or 30. . . . I got ten of them safe. I was very well satisfied."

Army Cooks and Kitchen, North of the Rapidan River Before the Wilderness, 1864

Cooks at Work

Group at Photographer's Tent, Camp Winfield Scott, near Yorktown, Virginia, May, 1862

Contrabands at Leisure, November, 1863

Sutlers' shops, forerunners of present-day post exchanges, were to be found in most Northern camps but were rarely seen by Confederates after the first few months of the war. These establishments dispensed cakes, pies, pickles, sardines, and sundry other delicacies, but prices were usually so high that private soldiers dependent on their army stipends could not pay them. More frequently patronized, especially by Confederates, were the farmers and Negroes who roamed through the camps selling pies, cakes, nuts, fruits, vegetables, and fish.

By far the most consistently rewarding sources of extra food were the premises of civilians who lived near the camps or along the route of march. The informal requisitioning—euphemistically referred to as "foraging," but more accurately designated as stealing —yielded a quantity of pigs, beeves, fowls, fruit, vegetables, honey, and other edibles that was limited only by the abundance of the supply and opportunities for getting at them. If Union soldiers were the worse offenders, the reason was not that they were greater rogues but rather that they were operating in what to them was enemy country and that officers and men commonly regarded the products of Southern fields and gardens as rightful spoils of war.

Foraging was developed to its highest point of proficiency by Sherman's soldiers on their march through Georgia and the Carolinas in 1864–1865. They had had considerable practice in Mississippi the previous year. Sherman's avowed objective was to impress on civilians the meaning of war and to weaken their desire and power to sustain the armies. This circumstance, coupled with the fact that his command traversed a rich country not frequented by either army, gave his men opportunities unknown to any other Civil War participants. They made the most of their chances. Indeed, the march was one grand feast, with turkey, chicken, duck, and other delicacies becoming so common that men actually were surfeited on them.

But Confederates, and especially cavalrymen, also preyed freely on both friend and foe. Governor Vance of North Carolina wrote to Secretary of War James A. Seddon: "If God Almighty had yet in store another plague worse than all others which he intended to have let loose on the Egyptians in case Pharaoh still hardened his heart, I am sure it must have been a regiment or so of half-armed, half-disciplined, Confederate Cavalry." A Mississippi infantryman stationed near Baldwyn, Mississippi, on June 2, 1862, wrote to his wife: "Our soldiers act outrageously, not with standing strict orders. . . . [They] have not left a fat hog, chicken, Turkey, goose, duck or eggs or onions behind." General Magruder in Virginia in 1861 and Hood in Tennessee and Mississippi in 1864–1865, had to reprimand their soldiers severely for plundering farms and killing livestock. Little wonder that a Georgia soldier wrote to his wife in July, 1864: "I had almost as leave have the Yanks around my hous as our own men."

A Texas private stationed near Little Rock wrote to his brother early in 1863: "The Government tried to feed us Texians on Poor Beef but there is too Dam many hogs here for that." This soldier apparently took what he needed without ceremony or subterfuge. Others, of tenderer conscience or greater imagination, were less direct in their depredations. Hogs and fowls taken by Federals were frequently classified as "strays," or unfortunate creatures abandoned by their owners. Confederates often justified their plunder on the basis of the alleged Union proclivities of their victims. And the number of pigs and chickens who forfeited their lives for such offensive acts as showing flagrant disrespect for the flag (Union or Confederate, as the circumstances required), refusing to take the oath of allegiance, or attacking innocent soldiers was legion. A favorite story told about the campfires represented an officer encountering a soldier with a freshly slaughtered shoat strung over his shoulder. "Soldier, didn't you know it was against orders to steal pigs?" asked the officer. "Yes, sir," replied the soldier, "but I killed this shoat in self-defense." "How was that?" "Well, I was walking through that thicket over there, when I heard a terrible noise behind me. I turned around and saw this animal charging furiously at me. So, to protect myself, I gave him the bayonet." Whereupon, the officer rode on; when he returned to his tent after nightfall he found a piece of fresh pork lying on the table.

Rations, however procured, had to be cooked, although on the march or in battle men sometimes were compelled to eat their meat raw.

Cooking arrangements varied greatly. The prevailing practice in both armies early in the war was for each company to have its food prepared by company cooks and served to the men individually or in messes. The latter were informal groups consisting usually of four to a dozen men banded together on the basis of friendship. Cooking and serving by company—undoubtedly more conducive to health than individual preparation—persisted to some extent throughout the war, especially among troops occupying permanent or semipermanent camps. But, despite recurring efforts to the contrary, the general trend was away from cooking in large groups toward preparation by individuals and messes. And this was always the prevailing arrangement during periods of active campaigning.

Preparation of standard fare was relatively simple. Veteran troops on the march cooked their meat on a stick, placed it between two pieces of hardtack or slices of bread, and washed it down with water from a canteen, or coffee boiled in a pint dipper, tin cup, or can. When the issue was flour instead of bread, soldiers added salt, water, and sometimes other ingredients, to make a dough and spread the mixture into cakes which were baked in skillets or on slanting boards placed near the fire. Sometimes hunks of dough were stuck on a ramrod and held over the fire to cook, or wrapped in shucks and buried in hot ashes. Confederates converted their meal into cornbread in similar manner; and many of them combined their meat and bread rations to produce a dish called cush or slosh. An Alabamian gave the following recipe for cush: "We take some bacon & fry the grease out, then we cut some cold beef in small pieces & put in the grease, then pour in water and stew it like hash. Then we crumble corn bread or biscuit in it and stew it again till all the water is out then we have . . . real Confederate cush." A simpler procedure was to fry bits of bacon in a skillet and then, when a sufficiency of grease had been produced, to stir in meal and bits of onion.

Sweet and Irish potatoes were baked in their jackets beneath piles of glowing coals. Messes pooled their rations of meat, potatoes, and onions to make hash or stew. Fresh or desiccated vegetables, seasoned with meat or bones, were converted into soup.

Most soldiers eventually became reasonably good cooks, and many regaled the home-folk with boasts of their accomplishment. A Federal who had just made "some very palatable doughnuts" wrote to his mother, "I wish I could send you one as a specimen of my cooking"; and a Confederate proudly informed his wife: "I will be able to learn you something in the art of cooking by the time I get home." Some soldiers became such expert cooks as to be able to turn out creditable offerings of pie—made from blackberries, huckleberries, grapes, and other fruits—plum preserves, molasses custard, baked fish, yeast rolls,

Thanksgiving in Camp, Thursday, November 28, 1861

roast turkey, and baked chicken served with all the trimmings and baked 'possum "chained with potatoes."

But delicacies such as these were rare. The average soldier was reasonably content with sowbelly and cornpone or salt horse and hardtack. Early in the war he complained often and vehemently about his fare. Sometimes he angrily threw his rations away. The grumbling persisted, but it gradually assumed the character and tone of habitual expression, uttered without feeling mainly to keep alive the privilege of protest. Hard campaigning stimulated appetites, and appetites adjusted themselves to the consumption of whatever was available. Quality gradually yielded to quantity as the matter of greatest concern. And this of course, was a vital part of the process of converting civilians into soldiers.

Clothing and Shelter

"And these poor infantry, artillery, and cavalry of ours, the more they serve, the less they look like soldiers and the more they resemble day-laborers who have bought second-hand military clothes. I have so come to associate good troops with dusty, faded suits, that I look with suspicion on anyone who has a stray bit of lace or other martial finery."

four

Company H, 44th Indiana Infantry, U.S.A.

The regiment was organized at Fort Wayne, Indiana, and mustered into service on November 22, 1861. It fought at Fort Donelson, Shiloh, through Buell's Kentucky campaign of August–October, 1862, Stones River, and Chickamauga. The regiment was mustered out of service on September 14, 1865. It lost 4 officers and 76 men killed and mortally wounded and 9 officers and 220 men by disease.

Plate 172 of the *Atlas To Accompany the Official Records* is a two-page colored spread, illustrating the uniforms prescribed for the Union and Confederate armies. Northern and Southern regalia are very much alike, for the military garb adopted by both sides in 1861 followed very closely United States *Army Regulations* of 1857. The principal differences are in the headgear (Confederate regulations specified caps) and in the cut and color of the coats. On the Union side, enlisted men, and officers below field grade, were to wear single-breasted coats; Confederates of all grades and ratings, from general to private, wore authorized double-breasted coats. Confederate coats were gray, but the trousers prescribed in army regulations throughout the war were light blue—a fact not generally known today. Confederates, with very few exceptions, seem to have disregarded the provision requiring blue and to have had their trousers made up of the same gray material as their coats.

Veterans who were still alive at the time the *Atlas* was published in the 1890's must have been much amused when they looked at Plate 172. For the uniforms displayed there bear only faint resemblance to what soldiers actually wore in the service. At the beginning of the conflict, dress on both sides was so diverse as to make mockery of the term "uniform." Many units started out for war in their fancy militia outfits, and some Southerners wore their civilian clothes, with perhaps a sash or a cartridge belt added, to go along with the shotgun, fowling piece, or dueling pistol with which some of them were armed. An Irish unit of Mobile was uniformed in dark green; the Granville Rifles of North Carolina wore black pants and shirts of red flannel; a Tennessee company known as the "Yellow Jackets" were appareled in yellow. On the other side General Sherman wrote of the Union Army before Bull Run: "The appearance of the troops about Washington was good, but it was manifest they were far from being soldiers. Their uniforms were as various as the cities

70

and states from which they came." As a rule once the companies and regiments arrived within the Union or Confederate training camps they were issued the regulation blue or gray. Nevertheless at First Manassas, Wilson's Creek, Shiloh, and some of the other early battles Union troops clad in gray and Confederates dressed in blue were fired on by comrades who naturally mistook them for enemies. In a class all by themselves were the zouaves of both armies who wore fezzes, red bloomers, fancy shirts and vests, gaily colored sashes, and white gaiters. On the Union side at least, some regiments wore their zouave uniforms up to the end of the war. On the day after Gettysburg the 20th Maine on a reconaissance through the Peach Orchard found thirty or forty dead zouaves of a Pennsylvania regiment who had been lying there three days in the hot July weather.

Considerable variation in dress persisted throughout the war, but the general trend on both sides was toward fewer and simpler garments. By the midpoint of the war a fair degree of standardization had been achieved, though this was less true of Confederates than of Federals. Writing in the fall of 1864 Theodore Lyman observed of the Army of the Potomac: "And these poor infantry, artillery, and cavalry of ours, the more they serve, the less they look like soldiers and the more they resemble day-laborers who have bought second-hand military clothes. I have so come to associate good troops with dusty, faded suits, that I look with suspicion on anyone who has a stray bit of lace or other martial finery."

After the shakedown period, the standard outfit of an enlisted Federal infantryman was a long woolen dress coat of dark blue with a high, stiff collar; a dark blue jacket or blouse, which for field service was much preferred to the dress coat; light blue trousers; sturdy black brogan shoes—the soldiers called them "gunboats"; a flannel shirt of dark wool; flannel drawers; socks; blue cap with black visor, worn with the crown sloping forward; and a long blue overcoat with cape. Artillery and cavalry dress was the same as for the infantry except that coats were shorter; boots were normally worn instead of shoes; and trousers were reinforced in seat and legs. In both armies each branch had its distinctive trimmings (red for artillery, blue for infantry, and yellow for cavalry). Branch was also indicated on the buttons of officers by appropriate emblems for ordnance and engineers, and the letters A, I, and C for artillery, infantry, and cavalry. Buttons of Union enlisted men were decorated with a spread-eagle design; those of Confederate enlisted men contained the number of their regiment, except for artillerymen, whose buttons bore the letter A. Branch was also indicated on the front of headgear by insignia and colors; Union officers and noncommissioned officers below the grade of general wore crossed cannon for artillery, a bugle for infantry, crossed sabers for cavalry, turreted castle for engineers, and flaming shell for ordnance, along with a brass numeral designating regiment and, when applicable, a brass letter specifying company; Union privates wore brass letters and numerals, the latter beneath the former, indicating company and regiment; on the Confederate side branch was designated by the color of the cap crown.

Rank was also designated by trimmings and insignia. On the Union side the insignia, worn on shoulder straps, was the same as that used in the American army of today. On the Confederate side general officers of all grades wore the same markings—three stars in a wreath on the collar and four rows of braid on the sleeves. Confederate colonels wore three stars without the wreath; lieutenant colonels, two stars; majors, one star; captains, three bars; first lieutenants, two bars; and second lieutenants, one bar. Noncommissioned ratings in both armies were indicated by two or three chevrons on the sleeve.

Kepi, Federal

Dark blue cloth, with a welt of the same around the crown, and yellow metal letters in front to designate companies.

Kepi, Confederate

Dark blue band; sides and crown light blue.

Sword-Belt Buckle, United States Army

Enlisted Man's Belt Buckle

Belt Buckle, New York Troops

Belt Buckle, Confederate States Army

Major Albert G. Enos, 8th Pennsylvania Cavalry, U.S.A.

Early in 1863 General Joseph Hooker instituted in the Army of the Potomac the wearing of badges—the forerunner of the modern shoulder patch—on the tops of caps and hats to identify corps and division. These were cloth emblems, about two inches square, of distinctive design for each corps and a different color for each division within the corps. The Second Corps wore a clover leaf, red for the first division, white for the second, and blue for the third. Various corps emblems, which were the same as those appearing on the organizational standards, are shown on Plate 175 of the *Atlas To Accompany the Official Records.*

The Henry E. Huntington Library has in its collection of Civil War memorabilia a metal identification tag, about the size of a twenty-five-cent piece, stamped "R. Williams, Co. G, 33rd Reg. N. Y. Vols., Buffalo." If this was worn by a soldier, he may have been unique among Civil War participants, since "dog tags," as modern troops call them, are nowhere mentioned in either official or personal literature of the time.

Among the Confederate rank and file the double-breasted coat was rarely seen after the first few months of the war. In its stead a short-waisted single-breasted jacket was worn; this garment does not appear among those prescribed in regulations for enlisted men; yet its use became so general as to fasten on Confederates the nickname "gray jacket." Trousers, a cotton shirt, drawers, socks, shoes, and a soft hat (which very soon supplanted the regulation cap) completed the average Southern outfit as of 1863. By that time the blockade had so restricted the importation of dyes that cadet gray had been replaced by yellowish brown or "butternut" as the prevailing color for pants and jackets. This distinctive hue resulted from a dye made locally of copperas* and walnut hulls.

Many rural soldiers, unaccustomed to wearing drawers at home, continued to regard them as superfluous during their army careers. Both Union and Confederate Regulations specify "flannel drawers" in the list of clothing allowances. United States Military Academy Regulations for 1853 specify "summer" drawers and "winter" drawers. Since no mention is made of material it can be assumed that both were flannel, one light, one heavy. It may be also assumed that "drawers" mean "long drawers." As the war developed Confederates preferred strong cotton rather than flannel, both because cotton was easier to wash, and because vermin did not propagate as rapidly in cotton as in flannel. But drawers as soldiers learned were a necessity to avoid chafing from the rubbing of the heavy uniform cloth on a long march.

Drawers had far wider use than the "stocks," which were authorized items of issue in both armies. These fixtures, made of stiff leather and fastened about the neck with a buckle, apparently were designed to make soldiers hold their heads erect. They must have been very uncomfortable.

The prevailing attitude of Civil War soldiers toward ties is suggested in an Alabamian's acknowledgment of a package from home: "I can put every thing to advantag except the cravat—If I was to put it on the Boys would laugh at me."

Authorized allowances—for a three-year period—of items common to both armies were:

* Ferrous sulfate produced by soaking pieces of rusty iron in water.

Item	1st Year	2nd Year	3rd Year
Caps	2	1	2 (1 for Confederates)
Cap cover	1	1	1
Jackets	2	1	2 (1 for Confederates)
Trousers	3	2	3 (2 for Confederates)
Shirts	3	3	3
Drawers	3	2	2
Shoes	2 pairs	2 pairs	2 pairs
Socks	2 pairs	2 pairs	2 pairs
Leather Stock	1	..	1 (none for Confederates)
Greatcoat	1	..	..
Stable Frock (mounted men)	1	..	1 (none for Confederates)
Fatigue Overalls (engineers and ordnance)	1	1	1
Blanket	1	..	1

Each item was given a cash value. Company officers kept account of clothing issued to each man, and soldiers who did not draw their full quotas were credited on the pay roll with the value of the articles due them at the end of the year. Those who overdrew their authorized allowance had the value of the excess deducted from their pay. Many Confederates, owing mainly to the inability of the government to provide what they needed, had all or a part of their clothing made at home. But among Federals, who usually were able to obtain from the government good clothing in ample quantities at low prices, this practice was restricted largely to "extras" such as vests, sweaters, fancy shirts ("red gingum" was the material specified by one Federal), handkerchiefs, and gloves. Apparently both Northerners and Southerners had to rely on the homefolk for the suspenders which practically all of them used to hold up their pants.

Neither government seems to have authorized summer uniforms as such, the assumption being that in the hot season soldiers would simply wear less of the regular issue. And this apparently is what most soldiers actually did. But a large number of Confederates obtained cotton trousers from one source or another, and in some instances these were worn throughout the year.

A good soldier, Union or Confederate, after he had felt comfortable about his musket thought mostly about two other items of his equipment, both of which were essential to his welfare and usefulness—his shoes and his hat. Shoes were always a vital concern as can be understood by the illustrations on Page 90, but equally important was the hat.

U.S. Army Regulations for 1863 prescribed for both officers and men, hats of black felt, 6¼ inches high, with a brim 3¼ inches wide. These were for dress wear, the forage caps were for fatigue purposes. Except by officers, the black dress hats were little worn even in the early years of the war. Later in the war soft felt or wool hats were adopted by many Union soldiers especially in the Western regiments. The Confederates had worn them almost from the beginning. In the autumn of 1861 a Tennessee Confederate wrote of the departure of his regiment for camp: "Nearly every body wore the Slouched Hat

Lieutenant John W. Ford, 3rd Pennsylvania Cavalry, U.S.A., at Westover Landing, Virginia, August, 1862

more for comfort than style it seemed to suit the free careless sort of the Southern man it was just the thing to shed rain or sun and a capital pillow at night."

A Georgia private wrote as late as April 30, 1864: "I have not got my hat yet. I need it very bad most burn up with the face blistered. I dont think I will ever ware another cap while I live." And Corporal Day Elmore of the 36th Illinois wrote to his parents on May 1, 1864 from Cleveland, Tennessee: "Father, if you can get me a light low crowned broad rimed fine wollen hat one that it will not hurt to do up and send by male the Boys get them in most Evry male and it is very warm hear I have nothing but my cap. I could buy one hear but they ask so much for them . . . send it as soon as you get this as my face is burning up."

Neither government seems to have provided an alteration service. Hence soldiers traded with comrades to get tolerable fits, turned up or slashed off long sleeves and trouser legs, or sent garments home for adjustment. A Mississippian recorded in his diary the following solution that he and an associate found for an underwear problem: "Dr. Tankersly had a pair of Drawers that were too small and I had a pair that were too large. So we cut a piece out of mine and spliced his. So we have got a pair of Drawers better for both."

Early in the war well meaning relatives and friends loaded the soldiers down with sundry luxuries such as sleeping caps; scarfs or "comforters"; mittens; and flannel waist-bands to be worn next to the skin as a protection against dampness and cold. Confederate regulations specified that "in hot weather a white duck or linen cover known as a havelock will be worn, the apron to fall behind, so as to protect the ears and neck from the rays of the sun." Many of these exotic pieces were lovingly fashioned by Southern women and presented to the volunteers. Some of the recipients dutifully tried to wear them. But after a while these and all other fancy extras were conveniently shed, and considerately reported to the donors as "lost."

Soldiers of both armies sometimes suffered from an insufficiency of clothing. Most of the shortages experienced by Northerners early in the war seem to have been due to shoddy materials foisted on the army by corrupt contractors who plagued the government during Simon Cameron's régime as Secretary of War. But deficiencies in certain items and at certain periods persisted throughout the conflict. Articles most frequently in short supply were overcoats and blankets, which soldiers had a habit of throwing away on the march, and shoes, which during seasons of active campaigning they sometimes wore out so rapidly as to overtax supply facilities.

The Antietam campaign rendered many of McClellan's men shoeless, and occasioned shortages of some other articles. A private in the Fifth New York Regiment, surprised and angered by Quartermaster Meigs's subsequent intimation that the Army of the Potomac was well clothed after the battle of Antietam, wrote to his parents: "I saw men with no coats, no underclothes, in rags, no shoes. . . . I remember when President Lincoln reviewed us that those who had Overcoats were ordered to put them on, to hide the rags and make him believe that they had jackets." The situation of which this soldier complained was not immediately remedied, for another New Yorker wrote from Fredericksburg on December 9, 1862, that two hundred of his regiment, the Second New York, were bare-footed.

The Gettysburg campaign took a heavy toll of shoe leather. On July 8th a Pennsylvanian scribbled in his diary, "a grate many Shiewless," and his complaint is borne out by official reports. A Massachusetts private after marching to Pennsylvania and back wrote to his

Captain Page, A.Q.M., Headquarters, Army of the Potomac, August, 1863

parents: "I am awful ragged . . . with a pair of pants on with a hole in the seat which like a broken window needs two old pots to stick through to fill it up." Soldiers who marched from Chattanooga to Knoxville and back late in 1863 to ease the pressure on Burnside apparently suffered more for want of clothing than any other wearers of the blue. A New Jersey private who was in this expedition wrote to his wife on December 21st that he had marched for twenty-six days "without a blanket or shelter, barefooted. . . . I wore raw cow skin shoes for ten days." Some of the troops who chased Price out of Missouri in the fall of 1864 and who followed Sherman through Georgia and the Carolinas complained of tattered clothing, but in most instances the deprivation suffered on these campaigns was of short duration and not accompanied by intense cold.

In general the clothing deficiencies experienced by Federals were far less serious than those suffered by Confederates. The men in blue had behind them the tremendous resources of an established nation, while those in gray were fighting for a confederacy whose credit was shaky, whose currency was constantly depreciating, whose industrial potential was limited, whose ports were blockaded, and whose transportation system fell woefully short of the demands created by war. More than that, the individual states, influenced by the exaggerated self-consciousness which had helped bring on secession, competed with the central government in the procurement of clothing and frequently refused to share what they obtained. In *State Rights in the Confederacy*, Professor Frank Owsley brings out the fact that while Lee's army suffered terribly from raggedness and bare feet during the war's last winter, warehouses in North Carolina were stuffed with great stores of leather and blankets and some 92,000 shoes that Governor Vance was saving for Tarheel soldiers, who were already comfortably clad. This was States' rights carried to a costly extreme.

Overcoats were rarely issued by Confederate authorities after the first year of the war. Many Southerners "captured" greatcoats from the Federals, but most of them got along without these heavy garments. Blankets were frequently unobtainable, and in the latter half of the war were almost as scarce as overcoats. Fitzgerald Ross, an Englishman who accompanied Lee's army on the Gettysburg campaign, reported that many soldiers carried blankets made of carpeting and that during inclement weather these vari-hued coverlets were converted into overcoats by cutting holes in the middle for the head and draping them over the shoulders. As opportunity presented, Confederates supplied themselves with Union blankets. Private Bill Cody was moved by a cold snap in late 1864 to observe: "If we do strike them Yankees again, they will get wone of the worst whippings they ever had for most of the boys are mighty anxious to get a lick at them for some blankets."

The clothing deficiency which caused Confederates to suffer most was that of shoes. And, as on the Northern side, the periods of greater scarcity coincided with long and arduous marches. After Second Manassas a journalist reported that Lee's army needed 40,000 pairs of shoes. This was probably an exaggeration, but there can be no doubt that thousands were shoeless and that this was a primary cause of the enormous straggling that occurred on the subsequent march into Maryland. It is entirely possible that 20,000 pairs of shoes represented the difference between Confederate success and failure at Sharpsburg.

Despite issuance of 10,000 pairs of shoes to the Army of Northern Virginia in the early fall of 1862, Longstreet's corps still was deficient by 6,000 pairs.

The Confederate Congress passed a law on October 9, 1862, authorizing the detail of two thousand soldiers as shoemakers, and this emergency measure, along with the settling down of the army in winter quarters, brought considerable relief. But the strenuous campaigns of 1863 in both East and West led to a new and greater crisis the following winter. In some companies half of the men were without shoes during the bitter cold of December and January. In December, 1863, one of Longstreet's men wrote from near Knoxville: "Mother you have heard of barefooted soldiers at Valley Forge, . . . but no men ever marched more willingly than did our barefooted men over the cold, hard frozen ground [here] . . . it is indeed an awful sight." In both Eastern and Western armies soldiers gathered up green cowhides from the slaughtering pens and made crude moccasins, fur side in, to relieve their suffering. On November 11, 1862, one of Longstreet's soldiers wrote: "General Armstad sent me a pair of raw hide shoes the other day and [they] stretch out at the heel so that when i start down a hill the[y] whip me nearly to death they flop up and down they stink very bad and i have to keep a bush in my hand to keep the flies off of them this is the last of the raw hide for some of the boys got hungry last night and broiled them and eat them so farewell raw hide shoes."

The clothing situation continued to deteriorate as Confederate fortunes ebbed. Southern troops experienced their greatest suffering in the winter preceding Appomattox. The soldier-historian of McGowan's brigade of Lee's army stated: "Clothing was sparsely issued, and what we received was coarse and flimsy. I do not remember the issue of a single overcoat and but a few blankets. Shoes were scarce. More than once a soldier left a bloody track on the frozen picket line." Even worse was the plight of Hood's men in Tennessee. A sergeant of the Forty-sixth Mississippi wrote in his diary on returning from a furlough in January, 1865: "I find my regiment—the whole army in fact—in a deplorable condition. . . . The regiment numbers about 150 men about half of whom are barefoot. All are ragged, dirty and covered with vermin." One of Hood's brigadiers in his official report of the Tennessee campaign stated: "During the whole time . . . [December 20–30, 1864] the weather was excessively severe . . . [and] for several days the ground was covered with snow. Numbers of the men made the march without shoes, some had no blankets and all were poorly clad. . . . What they had to endure was borne without complaint."

Confederates resorted to all sorts of expedients to meet these recurring crises. Uncle Sam was the South's best quartermaster, and a common saying in camp was that "all a Yankee is worth is his shoes." Many a ragged Confederate reclothed himself at the expense of a dead foe in the still of night following a battle; and some in the light of day compelled live prisoners to swap blue finery for butternut rags. Stonewall Jackson in May, 1862, found it necessary to issue a general order threatening with arrest "all persons found wearing articles of the uniform of the United States." After Forrest's raid through western Tennessee in December, 1862, Sergeant Tom Terrell wrote to his mother: "I saw our Cavalry . . . on their return; they were about six thousand in number and every man had a complete Yankee suit consisting of hats, coats, pants, Jackets and boots."

As previously indicated, the folk at home were often called on to supply clothing needs of the soldiers. General Lee repeatedly urged his wife and daughters to knit socks for his men. In the winter of 1863–1864 he delivered to the Stonewall Brigade 263 pairs of socks made by his womenfolk and their friends. On one occasion he reported to Mrs. Lee that he had recently been visited by a humble woman who had come to camp bringing her soldier husband a complete uniform spun, woven, and tailored by her own hands. The achievement of this woman, who had also clothed herself and her children with her handiwork, was duplicated many times over by Southern women. The clothing sent by wives and mothers was frequently more comfortable and durable than that issued by the quartermaster.

Both Federals and Confederates often took on themselves the repair of their apparel. John O. Casler, an amiable rogue of Stonewall Jackson's command, boasted after the war that he and a comrade did a profitable business half-soling shoes with leather surreptitiously cut from cartridge boxes and from the saddles of officers. A sewing kit, known as a "house-wife, was considered essential equipment by seasoned campaigners on both sides. Many boasted of their handiwork, though one Southerner admitted "puckering" a patch that he applied to his pants. Despite the best efforts of camp seamsters, Confederate uniforms often deteriorated to the point of being little more than a conglomerate of rags and threads. The clothing situation as of the war's last year was delightfully epitomized by one of Joe Johnston's soldiers who wrote from near Atlanta on June 7, 1864: "In this army one hole in the seat of the breeches indicates a Captain—two holes a lieutenant and the seat of the pants all out indicate[s] that the individual is a private."

Early in the war soldiers normally carried extra articles of clothing—along with station-ery, toilet articles, books, and photographs—in a knapsack. But in the course of campaigning most of them discarded their knapsacks and wrapped the contents, greatly diminished, in blankets draped from left shoulder to right hip and tied at the ends. Knapsacks, made of canvas, rubberized cloth, or leather, and strapped to the back, were only one of several "trappings" with which new soldiers burdened themselves. Some took along to camp drinking tubes equipped with filters for use in sucking water from creeks and springs. A few Federals, according to Southern reports of items found on the battlefields, equipped themselves with "bullet-proof" vests. Many Federals carried ponchos at one time or another, and Confederates appropriated for their use a considerable number of these raincoats.

The veteran soldier—Union or Confederate—considered himself well equipped if he possessed a blanket rolled in tent canvas or an India-rubber cover; a cloth or rubber haver-sack, known also as a "bread bag," which resembled an old-fashioned school satchel; a canteen, usually of canvas-covered metal, but those of Confederates were sometimes home-made wooden containers which had the appearance of flattened kegs; a musket; a leather cartridge box, loaded with forty rounds; a leather cap box; a bayonet in its sheath; a sewing kit; and mess equipment—hooked to the belt—consisting of a metal plate, knife, fork, spoon, and cup, and sometimes a light skillet. The weight of all this impedimenta ranged from forty to fifty pounds. A Union soldier estimated the weight of his own equipment thus: "40 rounds ammunition, belt, &c . . . 4 lbs; canteen of water 4 lbs; Haversack of rations, 6 lbs; Musket, 14 lbs; Knapsack at least 20 lbs; besides the clothes we have on our backs." Most veteran Federals, and nearly all experienced Confederates, carried considerably less weight than this. Elimination of the knapsack and reduction of its contents to ten pounds or less would produce a result that accorded more closely with established practice. Rare was the Southerner after the war's first year whose knapsack and food weighed six pounds. But even the lightest-traveling Confederate had to carry gun and ammunition, and he usually toted rations, water, blanket, tin cup and plate, and a few personal articles, and all of these added up to a weight of about thirty pounds.

Shelter for Civil War soldiers varied considerably with time, season, location, and other circumstances. When the weather was balmy or the army on the march, the men

Private Charles A. Pace,
Danville Blues, C.S.A., 1861

Captain William H. Inge, 1st Missouri Infantry,
C.S.A., Captured, February 10, 1862, and
Imprisoned on Johnson's Island

82

Group of Federal Soldiers from Maryland

often lived and slept under the open skies. Partly because of their prior mode of life and partly because of the Confederacy's limited resources, this ideal existence was considerably more common among Southerners than among their opponents.

The normal shelter, except in winter, was a tent. Corporal Samuel Storrow, 44th Massachusetts Regiment wrote to his parents from Washington, North Carolina, March 17, 1863: "I wish you could see us here in our camp of shelter tents. These are made in three pieces about 5 feet square, of stout drilling, one of which each man carries rolled up with woolen blanket in his rubber one. Two of them are buttoned together and raised upon two poles 4 ft long for the main body of the tent; the third buttons on behind like a sort of hood. The poles are secured by two cords which accompany the tents. Thus you have a tent which accomodates [sic] three brothers, who must literally be in-arms when they are all within. Shape, that of an inverted 'we' as Mr. Weller would say. Dimensions 4 ft perpendicularly and 5 laterally."

In the first months of the war, Sibley and wedge tents were in common use. The Sibley tent, shaped like a bell (one Confederate wrote that it "looked like a large hoop skirt standing up by itself on the ground"), was supported by an upright center pole. Its ten to twenty occupants slept with their feet to the center and heads near the edge, like spokes in a wheel. Wedge tents, commonly known as "A" tents, because from the end they looked like a capital A without the bar, were pieces of canvas stretched over a horizontal ridgepole, staked at the ground on both sides, and closed at the ends. The seven square feet of floor space accommodated four men with reasonable comfort, but when a half dozen were crowded in, as was sometimes necessary, they had to sleep spoon fashion; and during waking hours none of them could stand erect unless he happened to be of low stature and was near the ridge bar which was normally about six feet from the ground. The wall tents, which in effect were "A" tents mounted on canvas walls, were much more habitable than the Sibley and wedge types, but use of them was normally restricted to officers.

After 1861 the standard summer shelter of the rank and file was the shelter tent, widely known as the dog tent. In its most common version this was a two-man habitation made by buttoning together the half-shelters and stretching them over a horizontal pole supported at each end by a pronged stick or a musket stuck in the ground with bayonet fixed. Occasionally three or four soldiers would combine their half-shelters to make a larger tent; and if a man wanted to go it alone he simply tied the corners of his canvas to the tops of four upright sticks and crawled under. Shelter tents were designed primarily for sleeping. In warm weather both ventilation and roominess could be increased by lifting the entire structure three or four feet off the ground, or by converting it into a lean-to. During an extended period of immobility, such as was experienced during the sieges of Vicksburg and Petersburg, soldiers sometimes built shelters of brush or straw, either as extensions of their dog tents or as separate shelters. These could be occupied only when beyond the reach of musket or mortar fire or when by mutual understanding quiet prevailed along the lines. An outburst of shooting would send those in forward areas scrambling for the trenches.

During the winter months trench warriors took to "bombproof" dwellings which resembled the dugouts occupied by soldiers of recent wars. But the number of soldiers involved in trench warfare in winter was relatively small. The winter quarters of most Civil War participants were log huts or "barricaded" tents. Logs of the wall huts were horizontally

Confederate Soldiers

85

Private Francis E. Brownell, 11th New York Infantry (Fire Zouaves)

Soldiers of Company F, 114th Pennsylvania Infantry, U.S.A., Petersburg, Virginia, August, 1864

Sergeant Marshall M. McIntire, 29th Illinois Infantry, U.S.A.

Assistant Paymaster Meredith Howland,
7th New York State Militia

Corporal J. P. Goodliff,
22nd New York State Militia

Members of Band, 4th Michigan Infantry, U.S.A.

Federal Canteen

Confederate Wooden Canteen

Shoe, Confederate

Shoe, Confederate

Federal Shoes

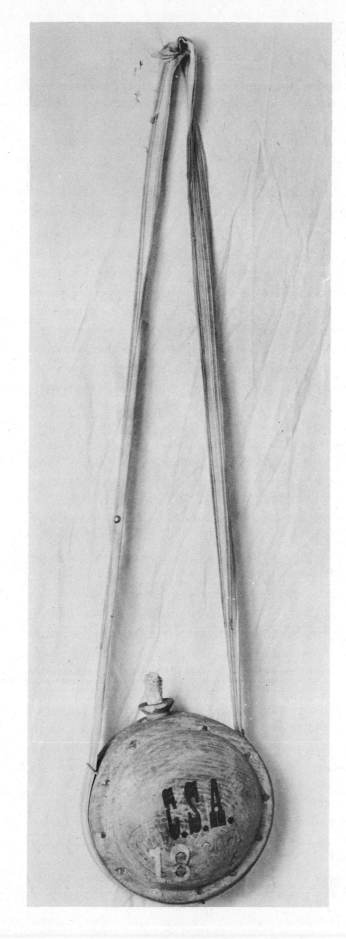

*Wooden Canteen Used During the War
by Private W. D. Smith, Company G,
47th North Carolina Infantry, C.S.A.*

laid after the fashion of frontier cabins or vertically arranged like those of a stockade. Cracks were daubed with mud and roofs were covered with boards or thatch. Barricaded or "winterized" tents were made by superimposing wedge or shelter tents on log bases. Like the log huts, they were usually occupied by four men. Spaciousness and comfort sometimes were increased by digging out the earth floor to a depth of several feet. Tent roofs were waterproofed by stretching rubber blankets or ponchos over the canvas. Heat was normally provided by fireplaces built of sticks and daubed with clay. Chimneys, similarly constructed, frequently were topped with commissary barrels to increase the draft. Soldiers occasionally were routed from their snug dwellings by the cry, "Chimney afire!" but the emergency usually was met by knocking the flaming kegs to the ground.

Most occupants covered the dirt floors with grass, leaves, or pine needles, built two-tiered bunks across one wall, and improvised stools and tables from logs, barrels, or boxes and placed pegs about the walls on which to hang their trappings. Illumination was provided by candles held in the neck of bayonets jabbed conveniently about the walls, or by slush lamps consisting of a rag wick protruding from a grease-filled can.

Almost every regiment contained a few eager and talented homemakers who insisted on adding plank floors, wallpaper, straw mattresses, shelves for books, papers, and daguerreotypes; chairs, and various other luxuries and adornments. Decorative tendencies sometimes extended to the placarding of huts and tents with such high-sounding names as "Astor House," "Santa Rosa," and "Lexington" (though some occupants used less pretentious markings such as "Growlers," "Pilgrims," and "Buzzard Roost"); applying fanciful designations to company streets; and erecting huge evergreen arches, with figures identifying the occupying units woven into the design, over camp entrances.

Whether their winter dwellings were elegantly furnished cabins or "gopher holes" dug in the sides of hills, the occupants usually managed to make themselves reasonably comfortable. The respite from hard marching and the remoteness of combat produced an atmosphere of relaxation and promoted a spirit of camaraderie. Letters written from these little cities in the wilderness not only indicate great pride in the homemade habitations but also reveal a degree of contentment reflecting great credit on the character and adaptability of American fighting men. The qualities are vividly exemplified by a letter which a rustic Southerner stationed at Fredericksburg wrote to his wife near the end of his second winter in camp: "You would be surprised to know how comfortable aplace I have to live in a white hous and a good fire place and a box, chunk on the ground wich are all used for seats hear we all take our seats some reading som writing some laughing some talking som set up sleeping and some thinking of home. . . . Mr A begins to tell whare he herd the first bum and how bad it sceard him and Mr B not to be out don tells what dangers he has pased through Mr C he tells his tale finely Mr E speaks as if Jest rose from sleep and says that he thinks he is the man that ought to have the next furlow F cant see why he has Enny better reasin for a furlow than he has. . . . H commences singing home sweet hom all the crowd Joines in." The talking and singing doubtless continued late into the night.

Over on the other side of the Rappahannock, other soldiers wearing different uniforms, but occupying similar houses and speaking the same language, were discussing the same topics, singing the same songs, and longing for the same things—peace, home, and the pursuit of happiness. Such men ought never to have fought. But they did; and when spring came they would reluctantly leave the calm and comfort of their winter abodes to get on with the business of killing.

92

Company D, 1st Rhode Island Infantry, Vicinity of Washington, D.C., 1861

Quarters of Captain Harry Clinton, Quartermaster of Provost Marshal, Brandy Station, Virginia, April, 1864

Officers' Quarters, Army of the Potomac, Brandy Station, Virginia, March, 1864

Young Lieutenant, C.S.A.,
Killed in Battle Around Richmond

Unknown Confederate Soldier
(Virginia Regiment)

96

Unknown Confederate Soldier (Virginia Regiment)

Federal Camp, Fort Wagner, Morris Island, South Carolina

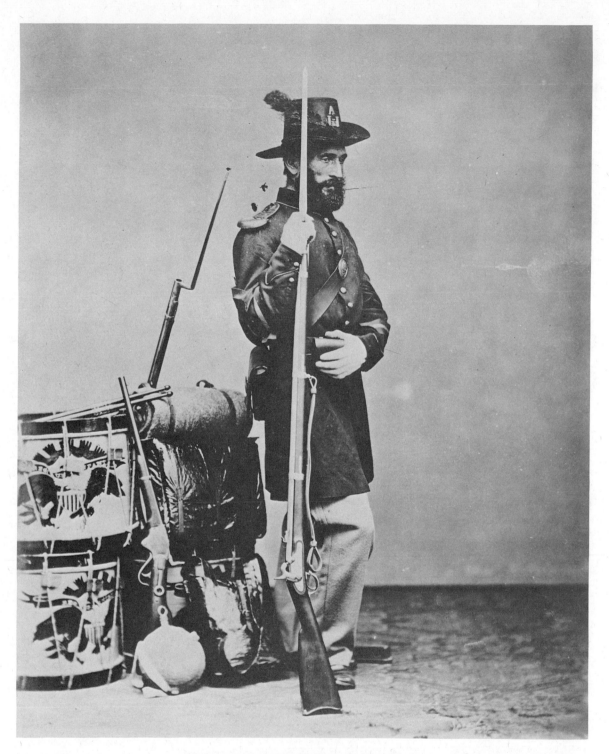

Noncommissioned Officer of Engineers

The soldier wears the hard black dress hat of the regulars, turned up on the left side and with a black plume on the right. This was the hat adopted by Gibbon's Iron Brigade composed of the 2nd, 6th, and 7th Wisconsin Volunteers, the 19th Indiana Volunteers, 24th Michigan, and Battery B, 4th U.S. Artillery. It is not to be confused with either the round felt hat generally worn on both sides for comfort after the first year of war, or the black felt hat prescribed by army regulations.

Weapons

five

First Connecticut Battery near Fredericksburg, Virginia, May 2, 1863

The Civil War has frequently been called the last of the old-fashioned and the first of the great modern conflicts. This is well illustrated by the weapons used. These included a considerable number of innovations. But the fact remains that the war was fought mainly with muzzle-loading rifled muskets. An analysis prepared by the compilers of the *Medical and Surgical History of the War of the Rebellion* shows that of all reported Civil War wounds 94 per cent were caused by bullets. Some of the "bullet" wounds may have been caused by the small balls contained in shrapnel.

The Civil War was primarily an infantryman's war; and most of the infantry were armed with either the Springfield rifled musket or its companion piece the Enfield rifled musket. Many other types were to be found on both sides, but these were the work horses. They were cumbersome and slow, but they were also sturdy, dependable, and deadly. They were called rifled muskets because they had the long, relatively thin barrels of the old muskets instead of the shorter, thicker barrels of the rifles proper which later supplanted them.

The Springfield rifled musket, named for the armory in Massachusetts where it was manufactured, had the greater use on the Northern side, while the Enfield, made principally in England but copied in the South, was the prevailing type imported by the Confederates. Figures compiled by the Chief of Ordnance in Washington after the close of the war showed that from January 1, 1861, to June 20, 1866, the Federal Government acquired 1,472,614 Springfield rifled muskets as against 428,292 Enfiields and 795,444 infantry shoulder arms of all other types.

The caliber of the Springfield rifled musket was .58. The length of the barrel was 40 inches; the total length without bayonet was 56 inches and with bayonet fixed 74 inches. The weight, including bayonet, was 9¾ pounds. These figures are for the 1861 model, but the slight modifications made during the war did not alter dimensions and basic characteristics. All of these models were equipped with elevating rear sights.

The effectiveness of the Springfields was proved by government field tests conducted in 1860. Ten "deliberately aimed" shots fired at 100 yards all struck within a space measuring eight by twelve inches; at 300 yards all hit within an area of 2½ square feet; and at 500 yards one struck within a target space of four square feet. In a rapidity test, one man, loading from his cartridge and cap boxes and firing offhand, was able to discharge ten shots in five minutes, and six of these hit a target of two square feet 100 yards removed; using a Maynard primer, an automatic capping device which eliminated the necessity of applying a new percussion cap before each fire, this man fired twelve shots in five minutes, four of which hit the target (two square feet) at 100 yards. In a penetration test, conducted at the same time, by firing at various distances into one-inch pine boards spaced an inch apart, bullets fired at 100 yards went through 11 boards; at 300 yards, 6.4 boards; and at 500 yards, 5.8 boards. In summing up the tests, the group which supervised them stated: "The rifled musket, of the calibre of .58 of an inch is a decided and important improvement . . . and considering the compactness, lightness, accuracy at long ranges and the use of the bayonet, the arm is in every respect well-adapted to the general service of Infantry." This report helps explain the reluctance of Federal Ordnance Chief Brigadier General James W. Ripley to consider and promote the development of breech-loading and repeating rifles. Ripley was convinced, and rightly so, that the muzzle-loading Springfield rifled muskets and their Enfield mates were good weapons; factories were tooled and workers trained to produce them quickly and in large quantities; many men were familiar with these guns and from manuals already available could teach the use of them to recruits; the development of effective new weapons to the point of quantity production was (and still is) a slow and uncertain process. So, Ripley, taking the conservative, simple, and natural course, concentrated on the familiar, reliable, and readily procurable weapons, and made them available to Union troops in large quantities. But all this is not meant to suggest that Ripley was free of slowness, blindness, and obstinacy. On the contrary, he was a difficult, stubborn, and unimaginative person who seemed to derive more satisfaction from showing why things could not be done than by devising means to accomplish them. As Professor Robert V. Bruce in his admirable book *Lincoln and the Tools of War* has indicated, with abler leadership in the Ordnance Bureau the Union Government during the course of the war might have done much more than it did in replacing good guns with better ones.

The Confederacy in its Ordnance Chief, Josiah Gorgas, had superior leadership, but it was handicapped by limited resources. It accomplished miracles in manufacturing powder and was notably successful in certain other areas of munitions production. Many small firms in the South learned to make a good quality of firearm, and the combined output of private, state, and national facilities was impressive. But throughout the war the South had to rely on outside sources for a large proportion of its weapons. Caleb Huse purchased more than 120,000 Enfield rifles in Europe, and in his report of February 3, 1863, indicated that at that time 70,980 of them had been shipped to the Confederacy. Nearly every battle yielded a substantial supply of Union rifles. All told, shoulder arms captured by Southerners ran to well over 100,000.

The Enfield rifled musket was caliber .577. The length of the barrel was 39 inches, the

A Confederate Bull Battery Previous to the Battle of Bull Run

over-all length without bayonet 55 inches and with bayonet fixed, 73 inches. The weight with bayonet attached was 9.19 pounds.

Federals and Confederates made surprisingly little comment, either in their letters and diaries or in reminiscences, about their weapons. The lack of derogatory statements about the Springfields and Enfields is in itself a strong indication that these weapons were satisfactory, for soldiers of both armies were quick to denounce anything that fell short of their expectations. The few comments that are available give them a good rating. James J. Kirkpatrick of the Sixteenth Mississippi Regiment noted in his diary on April 15, 1864, that he and his comrades had shot at targets that day with various types of guns and that "Springfield and Enfield Rifles generally do best." On October 17, 1861, Private Daniel E. Burbank of the Second New Hampshire Regiment wrote his homefolk: "We have not got the enfield rifles but the spring field they are just as good and a good deel lighter. We went out the other day to try them. We fired 600 yds and we put 360 balls into a mark the size of old Jeff. they will range 1500 yards with considerable certanty they do not cary so big a slug as our old rifles and are not as heavy by 6 lbs which is considerable on a long march."

Enfield rifles, commonly designated as "shortrifles" to distinguish them from the longer rifled muskets, were used to a limited extent in both armies. A Union soldier who drew

106

Battery previous to the Battle of Bulls Run

one of these guns in February, 1862, wrote in his diary: "Our Co. [K] and Co. A get beautiful Enfield rifle (short) with sabre bayonet. We are all right now."

According to Martin Rywell, a collector of Civil War weapons, "there were 57 varieties of guns used in the Confederacy with about as many variations." Many of the troops who entered the service in 1861 were equipped with cumbersome muskets, caliber .69 or larger, dating back to the early 1800's. Most of these weapons were flintlocks that had been converted to permit the use of percussion caps. Some of them had been rifled, but the majority were smoothbores using ball ammunition, either a single pellet or "buck and ball," which was a combination of one large and three small shots. The smoothbores were notoriously inaccurate, particularly at distances exceeding 150 yards.

One of the best of the older American-made guns was the 1841 (frequently designated 1842) regulation rifle, commonly known as the Harper's Ferry rifle in the North and in the South as the Mississippi rifle, from the fact of its use by Jefferson Davis' regiment of Mississippians in the Mexican War. It was 71.3 inches long with sword bayonet fixed, and 48.8 inches long without the bayonet. Its caliber was .54 and it weighed 11.83 pounds. Southerners were especially devoted to this gun. A Tarheel private wrote to his sister in May, 1861: "We received our arms. . . . Our choice was the Mississippi Rifles. They will [hit] good 300 yards." In the same month several Virginia companies, when told that they

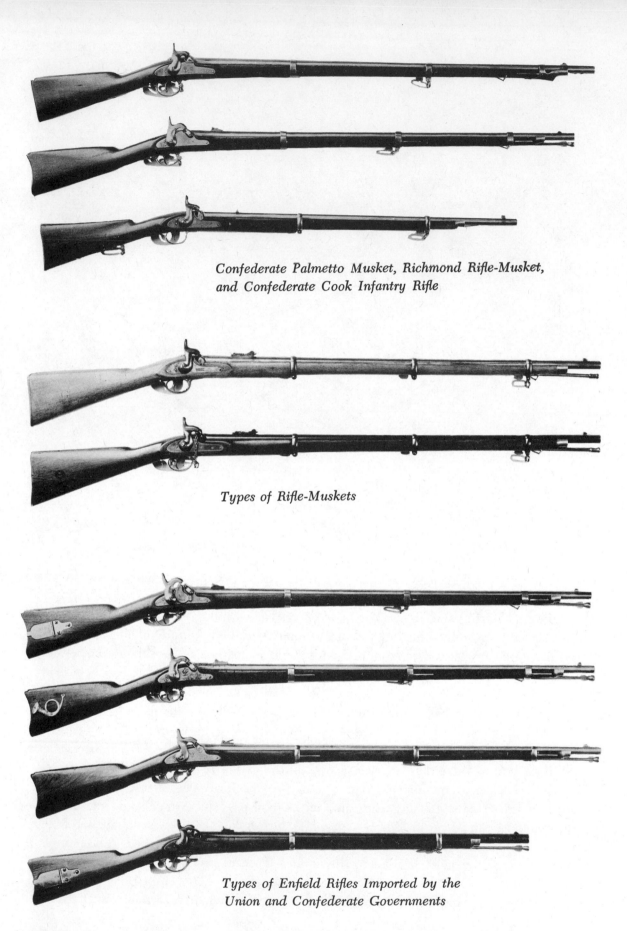

Confederate Palmetto Musket, Richmond Rifle-Musket, and Confederate Cook Infantry Rifle

Types of Rifle-Muskets

Types of Enfield Rifles Imported by the Union and Confederate Governments

108

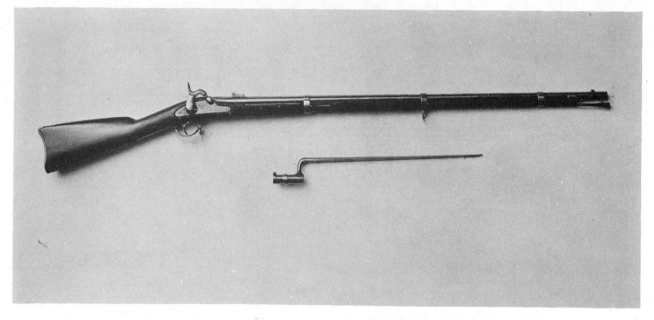

United States Contract Musket by Parker Snow and Company

were to be armed with smoothbores, threatened to mutiny unless they were given Mississippi rifles.

Both Union and Confederacy sent agents to Europe in 1861 to buy arms and on them were dumped, sometimes at scandalous prices, the offcasts of foreign arsenals. The Federals obtained 170,255 rifles from Austria, 111,549 from Prussia, 57,194 from Belgium, and 203,831 from undetermined foreign sources. Caleb Huse generally was outbid by Union buyers, but in addition to the large purchases of Enfields previously mentioned he procured about 27,000 Austrian rifles; and Confederates acquired by capture a large number of the guns imported by the United States.

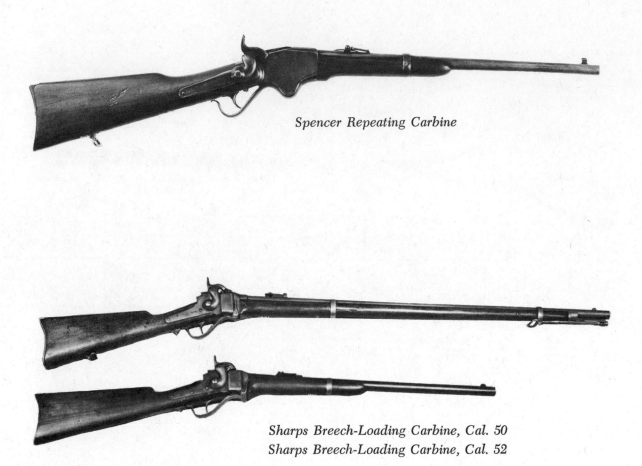

Spencer Repeating Carbine

Sharps Breech-Loading Carbine, Cal. 50
Sharps Breech-Loading Carbine, Cal. 52

Confederate Imitation of Sharps Carbine, Made in C.S. Arsenal, Richmond, Virginia

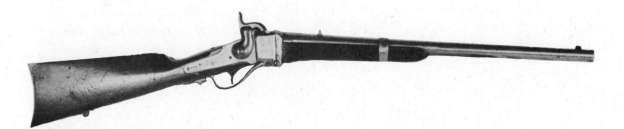

110

*Minié Balls: Top Row, Federal;
Bottom Row, Confederate*

Sharps Carbine Showing Breech

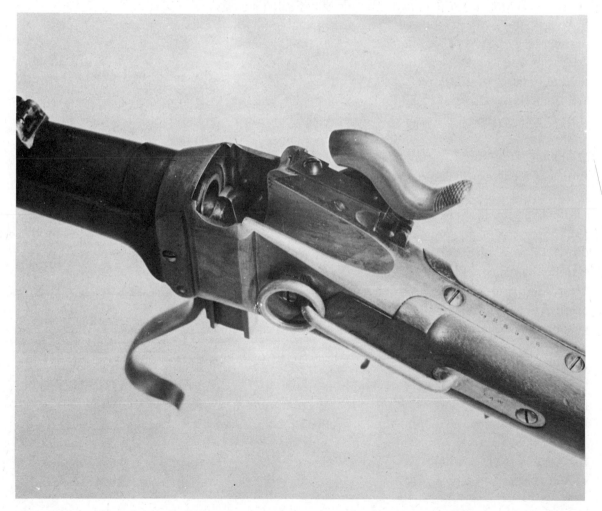

A Wisconsin private characterized the Dresden rifles drawn by his regiment as "miserable old things that . . . do about as much execution to the shooter as the shootee." And other soldiers made similar comments about the Belgian and Austrian rifles which were caliber .70 and .54 respectively, and so heavy as to merit the designation "mules" applied to them by a New Yorker. Sergeant Henry Buck of the Fifty-first Illinois Regiment complained that the Belgian guns "kicked terribly," and General Grant told a congressional committee that his men would hold the Austrian rifles very tight, "shut their eyes and brace themselves for the shock." Some soldiers called the Belgian guns "pumpkin slingers," and a young Hoosier pronounced the one issued to him as the "poorest excuse of a gun I ever saw."

Confederates had to utilize inferior weapons to a much greater extent than Federals. Many thousands of Southerners began their war service with shotguns, old smoothbore flintlock muskets, and sporting weapons of various types; and some of these were not replaced for a long time. At Fort Donelson the Tenth Tennessee Regiment was armed with old Tower of London muskets which had been carried by militia in the War of 1812. Half of the men in some of the Confederate regiments at Murfreesboro were armed with smoothbore muskets, and in September, 1863, about one out of every three infantrymen in the Army of Tennessee still carried the old .69 caliber smoothbore musket.

To get the best use out of the guns available to them, commanders of Confederate regiments generally gave the best arms to the two flank companies and issued the less desirable ones to those in the center. In some regiments arrangements were made for several degrees of gradation. Colonel C. Irvine Walker distributed guns to the Tenth South Carolina thus: Company A, Enfield rifles; Company B, Mississippi rifles; Company E, Harper's Ferry rifled muskets; the other seven companies, smoothbores.

Many brands of breech-loading rifles had been developed before the Civil War, and others were patented during the conflict; but owing largely to Ripley's conservatism (on June 11, 1861, he declared, "A great evil now specially prevalent in regard to arms . . . is the vast variety of new inventions") and to Gorgas's limited resources relatively few soldiers obtained these improved weapons. Against Ripley's advice, Lincoln on October 14, 1861, after a personal testing, directed the purchase of 25,000 Marsh rifles, but this directive was thwarted by the Ordnance Bureau. Single-shot breechloaders used by one side or the other included carbines bearing the names of Maynard, Burnside, Remington, Merrill, Morse, Terry (carried by General "Jeb" Stuart), Gibbs, and Star. Used more extensively than any of these, probably, was the Sharps (made in both rifle and carbine versions) which had won renown as "Beecher's Bibles" in the prewar Kansas troubles and which the famous Union sharpshooter Colonel Hiram Berdan strikingly endorsed in a trial witnessed by Lincoln in September, 1861. As he prepared to shoot at a man-sized target labeled "Jeff Davis," six hundred yards away, Berdan was told to "fire at the right eye." He shot, and when the target was brought in it was found that Berdan's bullet had pierced the pupil of the right eye. As Lincoln drove away laughing he called out, "Colonel, come down tomorrow, and I will give you the order for the breechloaders." But thanks to the stubbornness of the Ordnance Bureau, it was a long time before Berdan or the soldiers saw any of the new guns, and when finally they appeared they came in

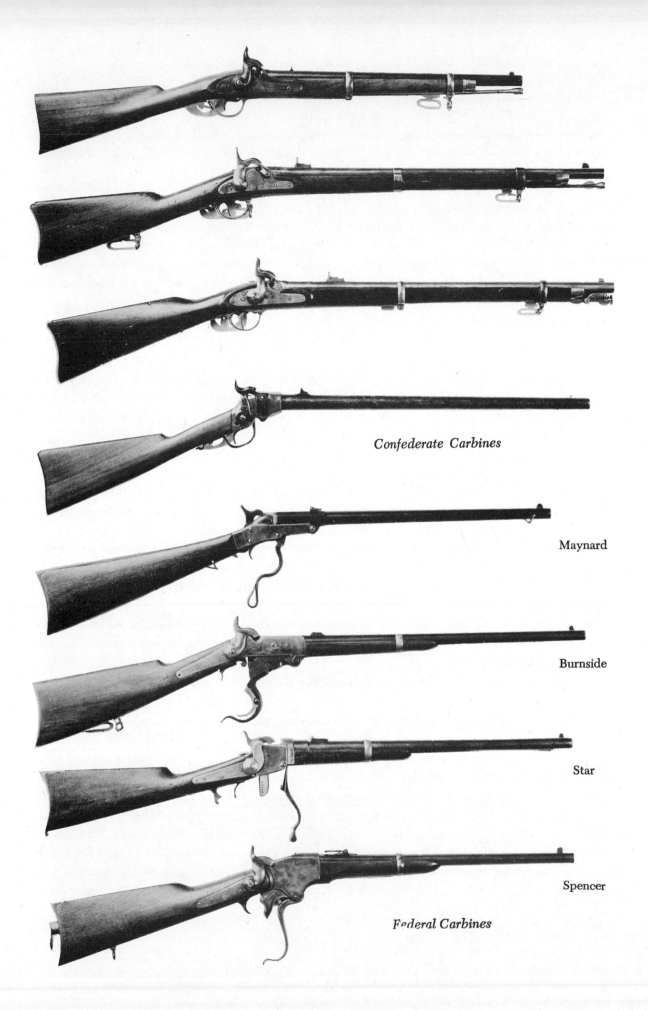

Confederate Carbines

Maynard

Burnside

Star

Spencer

Federal Carbines

driblets. The Sharps, which was copied by Confederate manufacturers, used a .54 caliber paper or linen cartridge and had a sliding breechblock worked by a lever. The Robinson version of the Confederate Sharps was .52 caliber. The end of the cartridge was sheared off to expose powder to primer as the lever closed the block. It could be fired eight or ten times a minute.

The most famous of all Civil War breechloaders was the Spencer repeating rifle, patented in 1860 by Christopher Spencer of Connecticut, and issued principally in the carbine version. This was a .52 caliber piece, carrying seven metallic rim-fire cartridges in a tube inserted in the stock which were fed into the chamber by working a lever. It was remarkably sturdy and effective. Lincoln himself put this gun through at least two trials on the Treasury grounds near the White House—on the second occasion he stopped by the War Department to ask Stanton to go along but the Secretary of War was too busy—and interested himself so much in making it available that it has been called "Mr. Lincoln's gun." The total number of Spencer repeaters placed in the hands of Union troops was about 60,000. These guns were used with telling effect by Wilder's "Lightning Brigade" of Mounted Infantry at Hoover's Gap, Tennessee (June 24, 1863), and at Chickamauga; by a company of Berdan's Sharpshooters on the second day at Gettysburg; by some of Rousseau's men in the Atlanta campaign; by the Seventh Connecticut at Olustee, Florida, and Bermuda Hundred, Virginia, in 1864; and elsewhere by other units. The Spencers did not win the war, as some enthusiasts seem inclined to believe, but they helped.

The Spencers made a profound impression on both their users and those who received their fire. General Bushrod Johnson, when confronted by Wilder's troops at Hoover's Gap, thought his brigade outnumbered five to one; and he suffered 146 casualties as against Wilder's 51. A member of the Seventh Connecticut Regiment wrote home after the Bermuda Hundred fight: "The Rebs made 3 charges on us but we stood up to the rack with our seven Shooters . . . and piled the Rebs in heaps in front of us. . . . The Rebs hate our guns they call them the Yanks 7 Devils they say the G. D. Yankeys stand up there with their G. D. coffy mills wind em up in the morning, run all day shoot a thousand times. Well they are a good rifel . . . & we are as good as a Brigade."

Another repeating gun, used to a limited extent, largely as a carbine, was the sixteen-shot Henry. A young Hoosier infantryman who paid $35—"all the money I had"—for one of these guns wrote in his journal on May 11, 1864, near Resaca, Georgia: "I got a Henry rifle . . . yesterday. . . . I am glad I could get it. They are good shooters and I like to think I have so many shots in reserve." On March 11, 1865, this soldier wrote: "I think the Johnnys are getting rattled; they are afraid of our repeating rifles. They say we are not fair, that we have guns that load on Sunday and shoot all the rest of the week."

The projectile used in nearly all Civil War rifles was the lead Minié ball (soldiers usually spelled it "minnie"), which got its name from Captain C. E. Minié, a Frenchman who figured prominently in its development. It was not a ball at all, but a conical bullet with a hollow base which expanded on firing so as to engage the riflings of the barrel. This snug fitting gave greater force to propulsion, enhanced the bullet's spin, and hence increased range and accuracy. Most of the Minié balls had grooves around the base in which wax or grease was placed to ease loading and reduce fouling of the barrels, but some, including Enfield bullets made in England, with paper bands attached, were smooth. The .577 Enfield bullets and the .58 Springfields were used interchangeably, but after a few

114

Color Bearers, 7th Illinois Infantry

The color-bearers are armed with the 16-shot Henry repeating carbine. The lower barrel is not a barrel but the magazine where the cartridges and spring were carried. The cartridges were fed into the barrel by working the lever beneath the trigger. The 7th Illinois fought with great distinction under Sherman at the Battle of Allatoona.

Percussion Caps and Confederate Paper Cartridges for Carbines

Carbine Cartridge Box and Paper-Wrapped Cartridges (Confederate)

Captain Schwartz, Sharpshooter, U.S.A.

Confederate Imitation of Colt Revolver

Colt Dragoon Revolvers Presented to Colonel George Washington Morgan by Citizens of Knox County, Ohio, in Recognition of His Services During the Mexican War

118

Le Mat Pistols Given by Dr. Hunter McGuire to General P. G. T. Beauregard, C.S.A.

General Henry J. Hunt, U.S.A.

fires soldiers equipped with Enfield rifles sometimes had difficulty ramming the larger balls home. One Confederate who was unable to get the bullet down, after knocking the end of the rammer against a tree, solved his problem by aiming and firing both ball and ramrod in the direction of the Federal lines. Even when the right size of bullet was used, fouling of the barrels by repeated fire caused jamming. If the users were patient and brave, they might remove the charges with little screwlike extractors which fitted on the ramrod, but apparently few soldiers were willing to fish for jammed bullets with missiles flying about their heads. The prevailing practice was to throw the damaged gun away and pick up a good one dropped by some friend or foe who no longer needed it. To guard against fouling, ordnance authorities issued special "Williams bullets" for use after every tenth shot. These were fitted with a thin metal disc which cleaned out the barrel on discharge.

Between battles soldiers were required to keep the barrels clean by occasionally washing them out with warm water (both ends were plugged with wood and the water was agitated by vigorous shaking) and scouring the inside with a rag attached to the ramrod. Regulations provided for issuance of muzzle stoppers known as tompions as a protection against dirt and moisture. If soldiers actually used them, they failed to mention the fact in letters and diaries. Exteriors of barrels and metal trimmings were polished with ashes, emery dust, and other mild abrasives.

Most soldiers received bayonets for their shoulder arms, but many lost them or threw them away. Some rifles were equipped with saber bayonets, so designated because of their swordlike shape and dual function. But the bayonets carried by the overwhelming majority of Civil War soldiers were the triangular type, held in place by a socket which slipped over the muzzle. From a ninety-degree elbow about two inches from the socket, the blade paralleled the barrel to the muzzle and came to a sharp point some eighteen inches beyond the end of the gun. Tactics manuals used by both sides contained sections on the use of the bayonet, and Federals had available to them a book on the subject prepared by General George B. McClellan. But such instruction as was given to the soldiers was almost a complete waste, as at close quarters they much preferred grabbing the gun by the barrel and clubbing with the butt. Analysis by the compilers of the *Medical and Surgical History* showed that of 246,712 wounds treated during the Civil War only 922, or less than four-tenths of 1 per cent (.0037), were caused by bayonets or sabers.

Many common soldiers armed themselves with pistols when they entered the service, but infantrymen soon learned that these weapons were superfluous. After the first year of the conflict the carrying of pistols was confined almost exclusively to officers and mounted men; and as breech-loading carbines became available, mounted men generally shifted to them as their principal weapon. Pistols used in the Civil War were of many types. Sizes ranged from delicate little instruments about as large as a pocket knife to pieces almost as long as carbines. Calibers varied from .36 to .70. Some were single-fire flintlock muzzle-loaders, and the opposite extreme was represented by the French-made Le Mat, carried by Beauregard, Jeb Stuart, and other Southern generals, which had two barrels one above the other and a capacity of ten shots—nine of caliber .44, fed into the upper barrel by a revolving chamber; and the tenth a round .60 caliber ball fired from the lower barrel. Among the brands used on one side or the other were Adams, Allen, Bentley, Cofer, Joslyn, Kerr, Remington, Savage, Starr, Trantor, and Whitney. But the most popular and

Union Shell, Parrott Type

Canister Shot—Fixed to Wood Sabot

Artilleryman's Tar Bucket

Whitworth Projectile

Hotchkiss Projectile—Forward Section of Hotchkiss Solid Shot

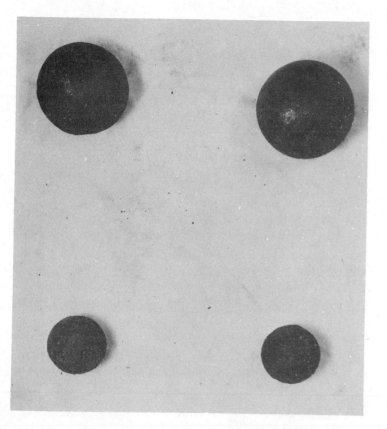

Miscellaneous Grape and Canister Balls

*32-Pounder Spherical Shell, Wood Plug Type Fuse
and 12-Pounder Spherical Shell, Wood Plug Type Fuse.
Probably Manufactured by Confederates for Use in Mortar*

Battery A, 4th United States Artillery, Culpeper, Virginia, September, 1863

This was Captain Alonzo Cushing's battery which stemmed the high tide of Pickett's charge at Gettysburg. On that famous day the battery was a 6-gun battery armed with 3-inch rifles. The battery was so broken up in the battle, and the casualties were so heavy, that in September, 1863 (the date of the photograph), it was reorganized as a 4-gun battery and rearmed with 12-pounder Napoleons. Thus the photograph shows the results of combat action and hard, distinguished service.

extensively used of all was the Colt "six-shooter." Southerners captured many of these excellent weapons, and Charles Rigdon and various associates manufactured a Confederate version in considerable quantities at Greensboro and Augusta. The army Colt was caliber .44, but the lighter .36 caliber navy model was a very popular gun among land troops.

Sabers were a part of the cavalrymen's and artillerymen's equipment; but, as previously indicated, these weapons did little damage in battle. The same was true of the swords carried by officers. The fierce-looking knives which were in such great demand among the South's first volunteers had very little use in combat, and the "Joe Brown pikes" which Georgia's fire-eating governor ordered for some of his troops were never tested in battle.

Small arms were backed up by fieldpieces of various types and sizes. Nearly all of the fieldpieces were muzzle-loaders and more than one-third of them were smoothbores. The work horses of the field artillery—and hence the counterparts of the Springfield and Enfield rifled muskets—were 12-pounder Napoleons and 3-inch rifles. These two types (counting 10-pounders of caliber 2.9 as 3-inch guns) constituted more than four-fifths of the Confederate artillery at Gettysburg and more than nine-tenths of Federal fieldpieces at the Wilderness. The 10-pounders were cast-iron Parrott rifles, caliber 2.9 or 3 inches. They were much less extensively used than the tapering 3-inch "ordnance rifles" which were of wrought iron and hence much safer to fire. By the spring of 1864 Brigadier General Henry J. Hunt had reduced the number of 10-pounder Parrotts in the Army of the Potomac to about thirty.

From the standpoint of use and popularity, Napoleons were the Number One fieldpiece of the Civil War. Federal ordnance authorities purchased 1,127 Napoleons during the period January 1, 1861 to June 30, 1866, as against 2,921 field guns of all other types; and nearly all of the artillery produced at the Confederate works in Augusta were Napoleons. These guns, named for Emperor Napoleon III during whose reign they were developed, were smoothbores, caliber 4.62 inches. They could fire 12-pound balls about 1,600 yards, but they were normally employed at much shorter ranges; and for close work canister was a favorite projectile. Napoleons were bronze guns, but in the latter part of the war shortage of brass caused the Confederacy to cast some replicas from iron. Napoleons were not so accurate as rifled guns, but their sturdiness, simplicity, and dependability justified the high esteem generally accorded them.

Lieutenant Colonel R. Snowden Andrews, the Marylander who is credited with obtaining from the Pikesville Armory near Baltimore the drawings used by the Confederacy in making the Southern Napoleons, early in the war demonstrated the effectiveness of the guns to his battalion by firing a charge of canister into a flock of ducks swimming in the Potomac. The havoc wrought on the canvasbacks not only proved the merits of the weapon but also provided the men with a choice Christmas dinner. Andrews's guns, commanded by the heroic Major J. W. Latimer, proved their battleworthiness on Benner's Hill at Gettysburg, July 2, 1863. And on the first day of that fight Federal Napoleons of Battery B, Fourth U.S. Artillery, rained destruction on Confederates pressing toward the little Pennsylvania town. As the men in gray closed in on his position near the railroad cut, Lieutenant James Davison limped about on a wounded leg, shouting to cannoneers of Battery B, "Feed it to 'em, God damn 'em! Feed it to 'em." And the canister hurled forth from the hot barrels cut gaping holes in the advancing lines. But the Confederates would not be stopped, and when Captain James Stewart finally succeeded in getting Battery

A Captured Confederate 12-Pounder Howitzer Complete with Caisson

First New York Battery (20-Pound Parrott Rifled Gun) near Richmond, Virginia, June, 1862

Mortar Battery No. 4, Yorktown, Virginia, 1862

B back to Cemetery Hill he found that he had lost more than a third of his men and nearly half of his horses. Manning Napoleons was risky business.

The 3-inch rifles fired 10-pound conical shells, and their effective range was about 2,400 yards. Parrott rifles, named for Robert P. Parrott, the man who devised their distinctive feature—an iron band shrunk around the breech to provide additional strength at the point of greatest strain—were of two field sizes: 10-pounders, caliber 2.9 or 3 inches; and 20-pounders, caliber 3.67 inches. The effective range of both was about 2,400 yards. Ranges have to be considered as approximate, since they were influenced by such variables as the quantity and quality of powder used, the type of projectile and the condition of rifling, and since the figures given in the various ordnance manuals are not in agreement. Confederates had their own version of the Parrott, the Brooke gun, named for John M. Brooke, designer of the *Merrimac*.

The 3.67 caliber James rifle, a bronze gun capable of firing a 12-pound shell some 3,000 yards, lacked durability and had only limited use. Confederates obtained Armstrong and Blakely rifles from England, as well as a few breech-loading Whitworths. The Whitworths were rated very highly for range and accuracy. They were of hexagonal bore, caliber 2.75, and fired a long hexagonally formed shell weighing ten pounds over distances estimated as great as five miles. The Federals obtained a 70-pounder siege Whitworth, and during the Peninsula Campaign they made some use of four 12-pounder Whitworths presented to them by some friends in Europe. But twenty Ellsworth guns, little cannon four feet long with a bore of 1½ inches, bought at Lincoln's direction in 1861, and contemptuously referred to as "jackass guns," according to Robert V. Bruce, "were the only breech-loading artillery purchased by the Federal Government during the Civil War."

Both sides used 6-pounder guns—rifled and smoothbore—in considerable numbers early in the war; but most of them were eventually replaced by pieces of larger caliber. The most famous Confederate 6-pounders were the four bronze smoothbores with which the Rockbridge Artillery initially was equipped. These little guns, which now have an honored place on the campus of the Virginia Military Institute, were named Matthew, Mark, Luke, and John because "they spoke such a powerful language."

Some of the fieldpieces were howitzers—short light bronze cannon designed primarily for firing scatter projectiles with medium velocity over curved trajectories. Mostly 12-pounders, they were effective at short ranges but were not as versatile as Napoleons. "Mountain howitzers," developed for use in rough country, were light enough (the 12-pounder barrel weighed only 220 pounds) to be carried on the backs of mules.

Much shorter than the howitzers were the mortars which came into wide use after the advent of trench warfare on a large scale in 1864. These squat pieces were set at a pronounced elevation to lob bursting spheres over into opposing earthworks. Most of the mortars were heavy weapons, but one type, known as the Coehorn, set in a wooden base, was light enough to be carried by four men. Mortars were extensively used on the Petersburg front during the final months of the war. At first they caused heavy casualties, but soldiers soon learned to watch the shells in flight and to scramble for cover before the missiles reached their targets.

Heavy cannon normally employed as siege weapons sometimes were used for field purposes. The largest piece used at Gettysburg was a 24-pounder howitzer, caliber 5.82 inches. Thirty-pounder Parrotts occasionally supported infantry attacks. In coastal operations, at

Brigade Officers of Horse Artillery near Fair Oaks, Virginia, May, 1862. Standing Left to Right: Edmund Pendleton, Henry Benson, H. M. Gibson, J. M. Wilson, J. C. Tidball, W. N. Dennison. Seated Left to Right: H. C. Gibson, A. C. M. Pennington, Wm. Hays, J. M. Robertson, J. W. Barlow. Seated on Ground Left to Right: R. H. Chapin, Robert Clark, A. C. Vincent, P. C. Hains

Artillerymen of the Mortar "Dictator" in Front of Petersburg, Virginia, August, 1864

Soldier Guarding Cannon at City Point, Virginia, 1864

Parked 12-pounder guns, "Napoleons."

Vicksburg, and in other engagements where siege situations existed, soldiers were subjected to the fire of heavy Parrotts, Blakelys, Jameses, Columbiads, howitzers and mortars, hurling huge projectiles measuring up to more than a foot in diameter and weighing more than a hundred pounds. In operations against Charleston, Federals employed an 8-inch, 200-pounder Parrott called the "Swamp Angel" and a 300-pounder Parrott which used a 25-pound charge of powder. Large rifled pieces which General Q. A. Gillmore used in the reduction of Fort Pulaski, garrisoned by Georgia infantry, in April, 1862, made history by demonstrating the vulnerability of even the mightiest walled fortresses.

Field ammunition varied greatly with the type of gun, the range, and the purpose of fire. If the range exceeded 350 yards and the object was the battering down of opposing works, the disabling of artillery, or the harassing of troop formations, cannon balls or conical shells were normally used. Cannon balls, both solid and explosive, were fired by smoothbores—most of them by howitzers and 12-pounder Napoleons. One explosive type, known as shrapnel or spherical case, was filled with balls about the size of small marbles. The little pellets, most of which were a half-inch in diameter, though some were .69 caliber musket balls, were packed in melted sulfur or resin. When the shrapnel exploded, these shot scattered over a considerable area. The spheres fired by Napoleons contained about 78 balls.

132

32-Pounders Which Shelled Marye's Heights from Across the River, May 3, 1863

The conical shells used in rifled fieldpieces were of many shapes and designs. They generally had some sort of device for expanding the base into the grooves of the barrel. Among favorite brands used during the Civil War were the Whitworth, James, Hotchkiss, Schenkl, Dyer, and Parrott shells. The manual for the instruction of Union artillery officers stated: "Spherical case ought not, as a general rule, to be used for less range than 500 yards; and neither sperical case nor shells should be fired at rapidly advancing bodies, as for instance, cavalry charging. The fire of spherical case and of shells on bodies of cavalry in line or column, and in position, is often very effective. To the destructive effects of the projectiles are added the confusion and disorder occasioned amongst the horses by the noise of their explosion." The conical shells, some of which contained small balls, were exploded by a time or percussion fuse placed in the nose.

Canister, the favorite projectile for close ranges, was fired by both rifles and smooth-bores. Canister was a tin can jammed with lead or iron balls, ranging in diameter from ⅝ to 1½ inches and in number from about 25 to about 76, though rarely exceeding 49. The balls were packed in tiers, in sawdust filler. Canister contained no powder charge, but was torn asunder by ejection from the piece. When hard-pressed by charging infantry, cannoneers sometimes rammed double charges of canister down the barrels before each fire; and the last shots fired by Battery B, First New Jersey Artillery, before pulling out

A Confederate Gun That Ran the Blockade

(the 6-gun unit had fired over 1,300 rounds—one piece had fired 241—and lost 15 men and 23 horses that day) to escape Longstreet's charging troops on the second day at Gettysburg were triple charges of canister. If the canister was loaded with 76 balls of ⅝ inch diameter, as one of the cannoneers later stated, this meant that each of these final blasts hurled forth 228 missiles; and scores of motionless bodies lying within the battery's range were a grim testimonial to the deadliness of the fire.

The maximum effective range of canister fired from fieldpieces was about 400 yards; and of double canister about 150 yards.

Another short-range projectile was grape. Authorities disagree about the extent to

134

which grape was used in the Civil War; some claim that it was not used at all by field artillery. A good many infantry officers reported that at close range they encountered a storm of grape and canister. But since small grapeshot and large canister balls were about the same size, and in view of the pandemonium that characterized the final stages of a charge, these officers could easily have been mistaken. Louis Van L. Naisawald, author of a definitive study of the artillery of the Army of the Potomac, states that "not a single battery commander from 1861–1865 reported firing a round of grape, though commanders often spelled out their expenditures in detail; nor is grape listed as a standard item of issue in ammunition chests." John Gibbon in his *Artillerist's Manual* of 1859 stated: "The use of grape-shot for field pieces has been discontinued for a number of years, it being considered that for the ranges of that kind of artillery, the shot of which canisters are made, are large enough, and the canister possesses the advantages of striking a great many more points at one discharge than grape. There is an advantage, too, in not having so many different kinds of ammunition." Grape may not have been used by Union field pieces; but it seems reasonable to conclude that Confederates, who repeatedly suffered from shortage of ammunition, on occasion dug into their reserve of obsolete projectiles and loaded their field guns with grape.

Grapeshot were arranged in layers, separated by metal discs and held together by a metal or wooden post running through the center. A 12-pounder charge consisted of nine shot, each about two inches in diameter, laid in three tiers. The cluster was broken up on expulsion from the cannon and the shot scattered over the target. The maximum effective range was about 800 yards.

Fuses used by Civil War artillery were of two general types. Percussion fuses, the simpler and more dependable of the two, were "caps" set off on impact by a plunger. Time fuses were of many varieties. Some, used mostly in the early part of the war, were wooden or paper fuses, notched to indicate time intervals (seconds) and cut to the desired length with a knife. Another type consisted of wooden plugs or metal screws and powder-filled paper inserts; the burning time of the fuse was indicated by the color of the paper: the black insert burned an inch every two seconds; red burned three seconds per inch; green, four; and yellow, five.

As the war progressed, metal fuses, which screwed into the projectiles (earlier fuses were tapped into place with mallets), were introduced in increasing numbers and by 1862 they had generally supplanted other types. The most widely used of the screw fuses was the Bormann, the outer surface of which was a lead disc with notches around the periphery indicating time intervals ranging from one to five seconds. If the range was 600 yards, the gunner punctured the 3½ -second notch with a punch, thus exposing a powder train leading to the inner charge, which would set it off over the target 3½ seconds after the piece was fired. All time fuses were ignited by the flame of the powder which expelled the projectile from the piece. Elongated missiles had thin umbrella-like cones attached to their noses which helped guide the flame of the propelling blast to the fuse.

Bormann fuses often failed to function properly, and objection to them became so great that the Confederacy, for a time at least, resumed the use of paper fuses. The Confederacy had more than its share of defective ammunition. Jennings C. Wise, in the *Long Arm of Lee*, states: "An extraordinarily large percentage of Confederate shells failed to burst

Solid Shot, Mortar Shells and Grape Amidst the Ruins of Tredegar Iron Works,
Richmond, Virginia, 1865

and many were even more ineffective by reason of premature explosions. . . . Ranging with the Confederate ammunition was extremely difficult . . . [and frequently] mere guess work. . . . It was most discouraging to the Confederate gunners to fire and fire upon a perfectly visible target under the easiest conditions and see not a sign of effect from their shells, and this is a fact which must be considered by the artillery student of the war." General D. H. Hill became so disgusted with his artillery equipment in April, 1862, that he wrote to the Confederate Secretary of War: "There must be something rotten in the Ordnance Department. It is a Yankee concern throughout. . . . Our shells burst at the mouth of the gun or do not burst at all." Hill's slurring of the Ordnance Bureau was unjustified, but there can be no doubt that some Confederate artillery was more dangerous to friend than to foe.

Artillery pieces were fired by the pulling of a lanyard. This was attached to a rough metal pin extending from a friction primer which fitted into a vent leading to the powder charge at the base of the cannon barrel. The tug on the lanyard, which jerked out the pin, created friction which ignited the primer, in much the same manner as a match is struck, and fire from the primer detonated the powder and sent the projectile on its flight. Gun barrels had to be swabbed out after each fire with a wet sponge; otherwise lingering sparks might set off the new charge as the gunner rammed it home.

Work of Civil War cannoneers was facilitated by the fact that much of the ammunition was fixed: that is, the powder charges (contained in cloth bags) and sabots ("shoes" which gave balls a snugger fit in the barrels) or wadding were attached to the projectiles so that the whole load could be handled as a unit. Rate of fire varied considerably with circumstances. The Federal manual of instruction for field artillery stated that "a piece can throw with sufficient deliberation for pointing two solid shot or three canisters per minute."

Confederate Torpedoes, Shot and Shell, Charleston Arsenal, Charleston, South Carolina, 1865

Despite the cumbersomeness of their weapons, Civil War artillerymen succeeded in throwing a vast amount of metal. At Gettysburg the Federals, whose guns aggregated 362, expended 32,781 rounds, and the Confederates, whose pieces totaled 272, shot about 22,000 rounds. These expenditures do not include the cavalry guns. Averages from the pieces actually employed (310 on the Northern side and about 213 on the Southern, not counting cavalry cannon) were 106 per gun for the Federals and 103 for the Confederates during the three-day period.

During the course of the conflict considerable experimentation was done on both sides. The results, while having only limited application during the Civil War, led to innovations and refinements which eventually were to help revolutionize the character of warfare. Northerners developed the "Union Repeating Gun," a single-barreled weapon, operated by turning a crank which dropped cartridges from a hopper into a revolving cylinder and hence was called a "coffee mill gun." Early in 1862, soldiers of the Twenty-eighth Pennsylvania Regiment in a skirmish near Harpers Ferry or Middleburg, Virginia, presumably used one of these devices to kill the first soldier ever to be slain by a machine gun. But George M. Chinn, in *The Machine Gun*, states that the Williams gun invented by Captain D. R. Williams, and employed by the Confederates at Seven Pines in May, 1862, was "the first machine gun to be used successfully in battle."

Land mines and grenades were used on both sides, and on February 17, 1864, a Confederate submersible vessel, the *H. L. Hunley*, manned by Alabama infantrymen, sent to the bottom of Charleston harbor the first battleship ever to be sunk by a submarine. Union experts tried to perfect rocket projectiles, but these never got beyond the experimental stage. They developed a flame-thrower, and it is possible that General Benjamin F. Butler actually used this weapon in battle early in 1865. References of Confederates to shooting down "moving bushes" in the Atlanta campaign indicate the use of camouflage by Union troops. Germ warfare was recommended by at least one Southerner; for on September 11, 1862, R. R. Barrow, a Louisiana planter, wrote to Duncan F. Kenner of the Confederate Congress: "I have been surprised that nothing has been done to carry the yellow fever into New Orleans. It could be done so easily by sending a man that had already had the disease to some yellow fever town & there procure fever corpse, wrap the dead body in Blankets & put in a metalic coffin. Bring the corpse over & then smuggle the Blankets into N.O. Thus started the fever would soon become an epidemic throughout the city." But no evidence was found of the actual use of germ warfare by either side.

Soldiers of the sixties fought their war with old-fashioned weapons, but the conflict stirred ingenious minds, put skilled hands to work, and initiated an effort which assured the arming of their sons and grandsons with instruments of destruction far deadlier than any the world had ever known.

General Joseph Reid Anderson, C.S.A., in Charge of Tredegar Iron Works, Richmond, Virginia, July 15, 1862

Diversions

six

The Irish Brigade Celebrating St. Patrick's Day in Camp at Falmouth, Virginia, March 17, 1863

Soldiers devoted only a small part of their time to active campaigning. Battles were infrequent, and few of them lasted more than two or three days. As a general rule the armies desisted from marching and fighting before Christmas and holed up in winter quarters until spring. But political and military leaders assumed practically no responsibility for easing the tedium occasioned by these long seasons of inactivity. They instituted no recreational programs and provided no service clubs, canteens, lounges, libraries, entertainers, post exchanges, or newspapers. Volunteer agencies in the South established some wayside homes for transient soldiers, and in the North the Sanitary and Christian commissions maintained a few rooms for reading and writing. But these facilities were designed primarily for the ailing or the sinful and offered little in the way of diversion. Soldiers of the sixties had to provide their own recreation. Fortunately the tastes of most of them were simple.

One of the most pleasurable diversions was music. On the march, about the campfire, at parties, and wherever else the men assembled, popular tunes were usually heard. Soldiers of the sixties were the "singin'-est" soldiers in American history, and more songs of the quality that endures came out of the Civil War than came from any other conflict.

Publishers in New York, Chicago, Philadelphia, New Orleans, Mobile, Richmond, and other cities issued vast quantities of sheet music and songbooks to satisfy the exceptional demands of the time. Collections issued especially for soldiers included: *Songs of the South, General Lee Songster, Rebel Songster, Songs of Love and Liberty, Stonewall Song Book, Beadle's Dime Union Song Book,* the *Camp Fire Songster, Little Mac Songster, Frisky Irish Songster,* and *Yankee Doodle Songster.*

"Home Sweet Home" seems to have been the most popular Civil War song. Other

A Snowball Fight at Dalton, Georgia

"We have had quite a fall of snow this week. It fell to the depth of several inches. It afforded fine sport for the boys. I never saw snow falling before. It first commenced by two companies then extended to the Regt. & Brigade. Finally whole Divisions became engaged. I did not participate with them. Some got seriously hurt, a great many came out with bloody noses, and black eyes, some lost their hats entirely."

old tunes frequently heard in camp were "Annie Laurie," "Auld Lang Syne," "Juanita," "Finnegan's Wake," "Lilly Dale," "Sweet Evelina," "Bingen on the Rhine," "Faded Flowers," "Pop Goes the Weasel!" "Listen to the Mocking Bird," and "Come Where My Love Lies Dreaming."

Religious favorites included "Old Hundred," "All Hail the Power of Jesus' Name," "Amazing Grace," "I'm a Pilgrim," "Rock of Ages," "How Firm a Foundation," "Jesus, Lover of My Soul," "On Jordan's Stormy Banks," and "Nearer, My God, to Thee."

Sometimes Federals and Confederates sang competitively. In January, 1863, a Virginia lieutenant wrote to his father: "We are on one side of the Rappahannock, the Enemy on the other. . . . Our boys will sing a Southern song. The Yankees will reply by singing the same tune to Yankee words." On a few occasions opposing soldiers sang together. When Confederate Private Goodwin got religion at one of the wartime revivals, about fifty of his comrades accompanied him to the Rapidan River for baptism. The assembly aroused the curiosity of the Federals across the river and a number of them came to the bank to view the ceremony. When the Confederates began singing "There Is a Fountain Filled with Blood," the Federals chimed in, after which the convert was immersed to the satisfaction of all.

One of the most dramatic incidents of the war occurred near Murfreesboro on the night before the battle of Stones River. Shortly after dark the bands of the opposing forces took turns playing patriotic airs. Presently one of them struck up "Home Sweet Home"; the other joined in immediately; and then hundreds of voices on both sides united to make the surrounding country reverberate with the wistful strains of Payne's immortal hymn.

Civil War soldiers were a sentimental lot, and this characteristic is reflected in their songs. "Lorena," with sad lyrics beginning "The years creep slowly by," was a top favorite among Southerners and greatly enjoyed by many Northerners. Lugubrious Yankee favorites which numerous Southerners sang with relish were "Just Before the Battle, Mother" and "Tenting on the Old Camp Ground." Of about equal popularity in the opposing forces were "When This Cruel War Is Over" and "The Girl I Left Behind Me." Of another sentimental number, "Who Will Care for Mother Now?" a Confederate wrote to his sister, "I think it is one of the sweetest things I ever heard."

Among patriotic and martial songs "John Brown's Body" and its moving companion piece "Battle Hymn of the Republic" undoubtedly ranked highest on the Union side. Other Northern favorites of this category were "Happy Land of Canaan," "Gay and Happy Still," "Yankee Doodle," "The Star-Spangled Banner," "Tramp, Tramp, Tramp," and "The Battle Cry of Freedom." The appeal of the last was strikingly attested by an incident in the Wilderness on May 6, 1864. A brigade of Burnside's Ninth Corps, had re-formed after a bloody repulse. A deep gloom seemed to settle over the unit as it awaited the word to advance. Presently one of the men began to sing:

> Yes, we'll rally round the flag, boys, we'll rally once again,
>   Shouting the battle-cry of Freedom!

His comrades joined in and soon the whole brigade was singing the rousing chorus:

> The Union forever,
> Hurray! boys, Hurrah!
> Down with the traitor, up with the star;
> While we rally round the flag, boys, rally once again,
> Shouting the battle-cry of Freedom!

The singing restored the drooping spirits, and the brigade marched forward with its accustomed vigor.

"Dixie" was the most popular Southern patriotic song (Northerners sang it too, sometimes with Union words, but more often in the original version), but "Bonnie Blue Flag," which consistently aroused tremendous applause when Harry Macarthy, the composer, sang it on tour early in the war, was a close second. James Ryder Randall's "Maryland! My Maryland" had a high rating during the first year of the conflict, but it lost some of its appeal when in the Sharpsburg campaign Marylanders showed less than the expected enthusiasm for throwing off "the despot's heel" and joining up with Marse Robert. "The Yellow Rose of Texas" was a favorite among Southwestern Confederates. Soldiers of the

Newspaperman

A Welcome Visitor in the Vicinity of Culpeper, Virginia, November, 1863

Army of Tennessee, after Hood's disastrous expedition to Nashville in 1864, parodied the last verse of the song thus:

> And now I'm going Southward,
> For my heart is full of woe.
> I'm going back to Georgia,
> To find my Uncle Joe.
> You may sing about your dearest maid,
> And sing of Rosalie,
> But the Gallant Hood of Texas
> Played hell in Tennessee.

Soldiers of the sixties had a good repertoire of humorous songs. Both Federals and Confederates made up ditties for the various bugle calls. William M. Dame, a boy soldier in the Richmond Howitzers, who later became an Episcopal bishop, stated that his comrades greeted reveille with a song beginning:

> Oh, how I hate to get up in the morning,
>   Oh, how I'd like to remain in bed!
> But the saddest blow of all is to hear the bugler call,
>   "You've got to get up, you've got to get up,
> You've got to get up this morning."

"Goober peas," a delightful Confederate song which satirized both a dietary expedient and a species of troops generally held in low esteem, contained the verse:

> Just before the battle, the General hears a row,
> He says the Yanks are coming, I hear their rifles now,
> He turns around in wonder, and what do you think he sees,
> The Georgia militia, eating goober peas.

Wearers of the blue had numerous comic songs, such as "Pop Goes the Weasel!" "Shoo, Fly, Shoo," and "Johnny Fill Up the Bowl." Both they and their opponents often made the countryside ring with the jaunty strains of "The Captain and His Whiskers."

In both armies Negroes provided some of the very best singing. Servants and teamsters sang individually and in groups about Southern campfires, and colored men who wore the blue entertained themselves and their white comrades with mournful spirituals born of slavery and stirring lyrics stressing freedom and Union. Thomas Wentworth Higginson, who commanded a regiment of South Carolina freedmen, recorded the words of a number of their songs in his diary. One of them contained the lines:

> Dere's room enough, room enough,
> Room enough in heaven for de sojer;
> Can't stay behind.

Another one proclaimed:

> We'll fight for liberty
>   Till de Lord shall call us home;
> We'll soon be free
>   Till de Lord shall call us home.

149

Holiday in the Camp of the 28th Pennsylvania Volunteers near Bladensburg, Maryland

"The John Brown song was always a favorite," according to Higginson; he also reported that the Negroes sang "at all times and seasons."

Another popular diversion was gambling. It would hardly be an exaggeration to state in scriptural paraphrase that "wherever two or three soldiers were gathered together, there did a deck of cards make its appearance among them and they did proceed to exchange their meager earnings." Favorite games were poker, twenty-one, euchre, keno, and faro. Excessive use caused cards to wear out quickly, and Confederates had a hard time replacing them after paper became scarce. In some instances gambling wearers of the gray played with homemade cards fashioned from heavy paper.

Soldiers "shot craps" and rolled dice in a banking game known as chuck-a-luck.* They

* Chuck-a-luck, known also as sweet-cloth and bird-cage, was an old game of uncertain origin, played by rolling three dice from a cup, the players betting on the numbers that would turn up. The game was described thus in a newspaper: "a lot of fellows mark off numbers 1-2-3-4-5-6, put the money on the numbers and throw dice, and the fellow's numbers turned up take the pot." See W. A. Craigie and J. R. Hulbert, *A Dictionary of American English* (Chicago, 1938), I, 501.

Ft. Totten.

Fort Hill

Holiday in the camp of the 23 Penn. Vol. near Bladensburg.

climbing a greased pole

raffled off watches, knives, rings, coats, blankets, and sundry other articles. Much money was lost and won on horse races, cockfights, and wrestling matches. Men of Joe Johnston's army, hard-pressed for gambling devices, utilized camp lice for gambling purposes. The procedure in the First Tennessee Regiment, according to Private Sam Watkins, was for each contestant to lay a tin plate on the ground, bottom up, and place a louse in the center of it. The soldier whose louse first vacated the plate was adjudged the winner. In a series of contests, Watkins stated, the louse run by Private Dornin won so consistently that the other participants became suspicious. An investigation revealed that Dornin had been heating his plate before each contest, thus inciting his louse to exceptional effort.

Gambling was an especially popular activity on payday, and many officers and men quickly lost all their earnings. A Tennessee colonel whose regiment received six months' pay in September, 1862, wrote that immediately after the money was dispensed one of the privates set up a chuck-a-luck board and in very short order stripped some of his comrades of all that they had received.

Sutler's Tent, 1st Brigade Horse Artillery, U.S.A.

Sutler's Tent, 2nd Division, 9th Army Corps, November, 1864

Fruit and Oyster House in Front of Petersburg, Virginia, 1864 (Bombproof Soldiers' Restaurant)

The lure of chance was so great that soldiers gambled under every conceivable circumstance. A Mississippian wrote his homefolk: "Yesterday was Sunday and I sat at my fire and saw the preachers holding forth about thirty steps off and between them and me were two games of poker, where each one was trying to fill his pockets at the expense of his neighbor." Occasionally men would shuffle and deal in full action. But hell-fire was too much of a reality to men steeped in mid-nineteenth century orthodoxy to permit wide indulgence in this sort of thing. Many men on both sides threw their cards away as they advanced to battle, dreading to be struck down with instruments of sin on their persons. But if they survived they usually tried to recover their discarded treasures.

Many soldiers found diversion in reading. Because of their better educational background and their easier access to books and papers, Federals read far more than Confederates. Newspapers which were regularly hawked in most Northern camps for five to ten cents an issue were much more widely read than any other type of literature; and picture papers, such as *Frank Leslie's*, were the most popular of all. Magazines such as the *North American Review*, the *Atlantic*, and *Harper's* had considerable circulation in Northern camps, and a good many Confederates read the *Southern Illustrated News, Field and Fireside* and the *Southern Literary Messenger*. Shakespeare, Milton, Horace, Victor Hugo, Dumas, Bulwer-Lytton, Swift, Scott, and Cooper had avid readers in both camps, and a few pored over the original Latin and Greek of the ancient classics. But a far greater number devoted their leisure to "Bill Arp," "Mr. Dooley," "Phunny Fellow," "Nix-Nax," "Budget of Fun," and especially Beadle's "Dime Novels." On both sides, the Bible seems to have been the most widely read book.

Baseball flourished in both Northern and Southern camps. Sticks and planks often served as bats, and the ball sometimes was a yarn-covered walnut. But this was no damper to enthusiasm. An Alabama captain wrote that Joe Johnston's soldiers encamped at Dalton, Georgia, early in 1864 "played baseball just like school boys," and a game played by Union troops at Hiltonhead, South Carolina, on Christmas Day, 1862, was said to have attracted a crowd of 40,000 soldiers and civilians. The sports most commonly enjoyed were boxing, foot races, leapfrog, broad jumping, and free-for-all scuffles in which whole regiments participated, including snowball fights.

Soldiers whiled away many hours at cards, checkers, and dominoes; and almost every camp had a few chess addicts. Horse racing and cockfighting provided entertainment for some, but a far greater number found diversion in practical jokes. Raw recruits, naïve civilians and colored camp followers were the most frequent victims of banter and horseplay. One day a seedy-looking farmer appeared in a Confederate camp inquiring for a lost mule. Word of the poor man's plight spread through the camp, and from down the tent row came the cry, "Here's your mule!" The farmer ambled hopefully to the point whence the shout came, but could find no one who had seen the stray. Then, in another part of the camp the cry was raised, "Here's your mule!" with similar result; and presently the whole area was resounding with the call. Thus was originated a saying which gained wide currency in the Southern army.

Thanksgiving, Christmas, Fourth of July, and other festive occasions were nearly always enlivened by music, drinking (officers, who had the exclusive privilege of buying spirits from the commissary, often furnished the "Oh Be Joyful"), and dancing. When feminine partners were not available, which was usually the case, some of the soldiers donned feminine attire and acted as substitutes. As may well be imagined, festivities frequently were rowdy and some of them degenerated into rampant brawls. An Illinois sergeant wrote after a regimental Christmas spree in 1864: "Col. Tom turned out 15 *galls* of Rotgut & several of the boys got Happy and some got pugilistic, and as a consequence some had Eyes Red & some black and all felt as though they had been poorly staid with."

Soldiers who belonged to the Masonic order or other fraternal organizations sometimes

Night Amusements in a Confederate Camp

Mrs. Kate Chase Sprague Who Attended the Washington's Birthday Ball

Washington's Birthday Ball at Corps Headquarters, Brandy Station, Virginia, February 22, 1864

"The ball was a compliment to the many ladies; families of the officers, who were in camp, and many more came down from Washington for the occasion. It was a very brilliant affair, to which the handsome dresses of the ladies and the showy uniforms of the officers, greatly contributed. No thought was given to the dangers of the past, or those of the near future; but all gave themselves up to the enjoyment of the hour."—Joseph R. C. Ward, *History of the One Hundred and Sixth Regiment Pennsylvania Volunteers.*

got together for meetings. Men of forensic inclinations formed literary and debating societies and discussed topics ranging from the serious to the ridiculous. One Federal group argued the proposition, "Resolved: That the Present War will be More Productive of Good than Evil." Another considered "Which Has the Most Influence on Men, to-wit Money or Woman?" and decided in favor of woman. Still a third, after earnestly debating for one and one-half hours the question of whether or not intemperance was a greater evil than war, concluded that Bacchus held the edge over Mars.

Drama was a source of entertainment for many. Soldiers stationed near towns and cities occasionally attended the offerings of professional casts. But the great majority were restricted to camp productions staged by soldiers. Sometimes performances were given in the open air on rough stages and with meager properties before audiences sitting on log benches or lolling on the ground. But when circumstances permitted, arrangements might be elaborate. The Forty-fourth Massachusetts Regiment, made up largely of men from the Boston area, had a dramatic organization which presented a series of highly creditable performances. One of their shows featured the trial scene from *The Merchant of Venice*. Among Confederates the Battalion of Washington Artillery of New Orleans boasted one of the most talented theatrical groups. During the winter of 1862–1863, while the battalion was stationed near Fredericksburg, its players presented several variety shows for which printed programs were prepared and widely distributed. A special train brought a large crowd from Richmond to see one performance; Longstreet and other generals came in resplendent uniforms; and common soldiers flocked in from points as far removed as twenty miles. The feature of this show was a farce entitled "Pocahontas, or Ye Gentle Savage."

Minstrels and comedies were the principal offerings. Especially popular with the soldier audiences were presentations satirizing camp routine, rations, officers, and surgeons. Actors of the Stonewall and Louisiana brigades brought down the house with "The Medical Board," a skit which showed a group of surgeons in consultation, drinking whisky sent to camp for the exclusive use of sick soldiers and then deciding first to lop off a wounded man's arms, then his legs, and finally his head. To the patient's inquiry after each decision, "Can I have a furlough?" the doctors replied, "No, your services are indispensable." When told that his head must be amputated, he said, "Then I know I can have a furlough." But the chief surgeon replied: "We are so scarce of men that your body will have to be set up in the breastworks to fool the enemy."

Handicraft helped many soldiers while away long periods of inactivity in camp, hospital and prison. Pipes were carved from brierroot and chessmen from pine and sassafras. Rings were fashioned from bones and uniform buttons. Leaden Minie balls were converted into miniature soldiers and sundry other trifles. And strips from commissary boxes were trimmed into all sorts of shapes and patterns or reduced to piles of shavings solely for the pleasure of whittling.

Soldiers of journalistic bent occasionally diverted themselves and their associates by issuing unit newspapers. Because the Northern ranks contained many more printers and because of their more favorable circumstances, Federals published several times as many of these camp sheets as did their opponents. When a Union regiment occupied a Southern

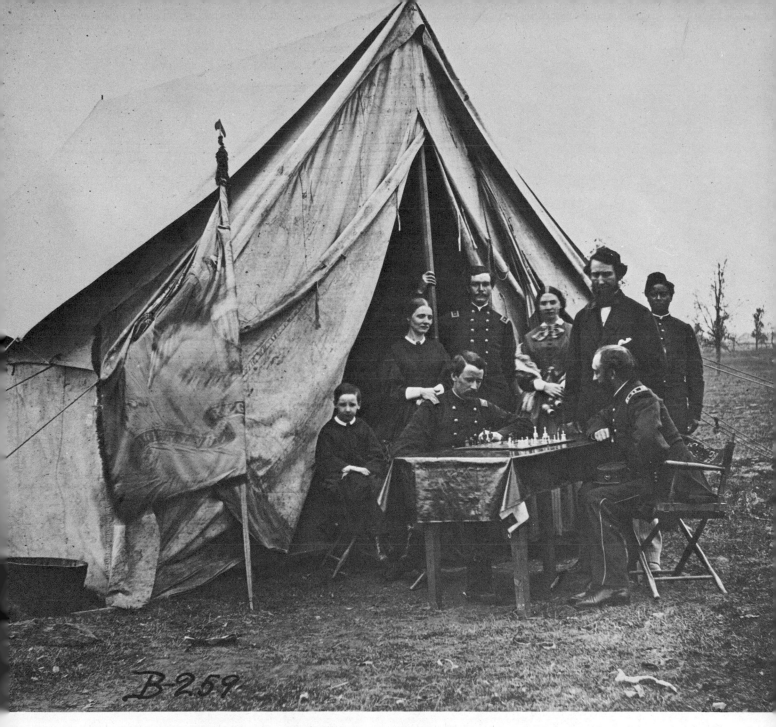

Colonel James P. McMahon and Friends Playing Chess at Headquarters of 164th New York Infantry, U.S.A.

Captain Samuel W. Owen, 3rd Pennsylvania Cavalry, Caught Napping at Westover Landing, Virginia, August, 1862

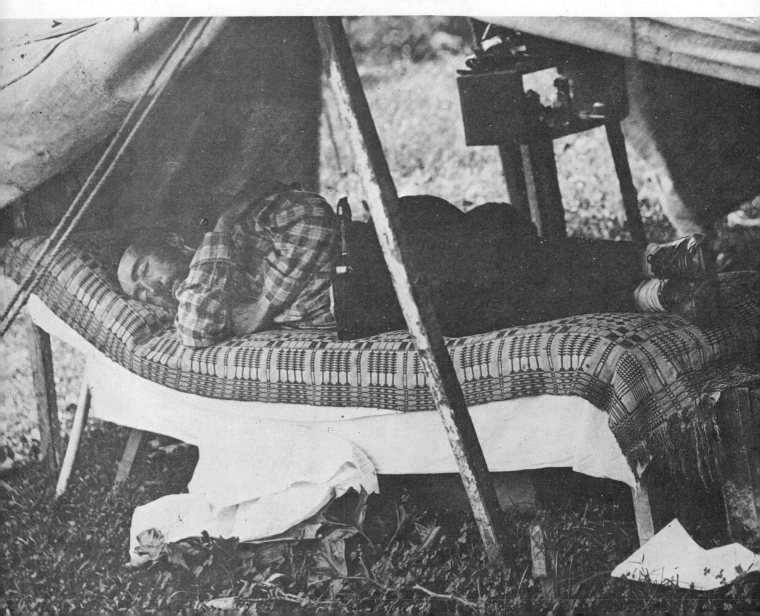

town, printers usually made a beeline for the newspaper office. If the type, press, and newsprint had not been destroyed or removed, and the situation permitted, they ran off a paper of one or more pages in which they announced their arrival, recounted recent happenings in the command, related a few anecdotes, and threw in a few verses and fake ads for filler. The papers were distributed among comrades and a few copies mailed to friends and relatives at home. Confederates, operating nearly always in friendly country, usually had to depend on borrowing the facilities of some local printer, though John Morgan's men had the good fortune of finding an abandoned press in Hartsville, Tennessee, which they appropriated and carried about with them to publish the *Vidette*.

Sometimes the soldier-journalists gave the camp papers the name of their unit, as did those who published the *First Minnesota*, the *Connecticut Fifth*, and the *Pennsylvania Thirteenth*. In other instances they chose titles suggested by popular leaders, patriotic sentiment, or camp life, such as *Unconditional S. Grant*, *Lauman's Own*, *Buck and Ball*, *Camp Kettle*, and *Camp Hudson Times*.

If facilities for printing were not available, soldiers sometimes wrote out small papers for limited distribution. Examples of manuscript sheets are the "Pioneer Banner," published "semi-occasionally for the young ladies of the Union Female College" by young Confederates stationed at Fort Barrancas, and the "Secesh Eradicator" edited by "Bayonette" for the Eighty-fifth Illinois Regiment.

Most camp papers did not last beyond one or two issues, though some ran for several months. The total number of known titles on both sides ran to more than two hundred.

But the diversion that afforded the greatest pleasure to every man in all the armies was a letter from home. "A letter from home is to me like food to the hungry and rest to the weary," wrote a Maine private to his wife in January, 1863. About the same time an Alabamian wrote his spouse: "Martha I waunt you to Write often and send me all the nuse for I am one of the Glades fellowes that you Ever seen When I Git a letter from you. You dont no now much good it dus me."

The cry "Come get your mail" was the most thrilling call ever heard in camp. Response to the welcome announcement took precedence over every other activity, even eating. "Boys who will lie upon their backs with hardly energy enough to turn over will jump up and hurry to the captain's tent when mail call is sounded," wrote an Alabamian to his wife. An Ohio soldier in describing receipt of mail by his regiment stated that "it made the boys shout with joy to heare from home once more." And another Federal on hearing from his homefolk after a long interruption of mail service, wrote in reply: "I can never remember of having been so glad before. I cried with joy and thankfulness."

Soldiers importuned the homefolk to write them often. They preferred long letters, but the principal concern was frequency. One Northerner wrote teasingly to his spouse: "Yore leter was short and sweet jist like a rosted maget."

The most satisfying missives were those that were full of detail about the minutiae of home affairs—how many teeth the baby had cut; what new tricks the children had learned; what fruits were in season; how the crops progressed; what gossip circulated in the community; and who was courting the Widow Jones. These and all other bits of news soldiers of both armies longed to hear. But the important thing was to hear *something*. "FOR GOD SAKE RITE" was the oft-repeated plea of one Northerner to his parents, and he expressed an all-pervasive sentiment. In some instances letters were kept, read, and reread until from hard use they fell apart.

Crime and Punishment

seven

*Stockade of 50th New York
Engineers, Rappahannock
Station, Virginia,
March, 1864*

Just as civil society requires a code of municipal law "commanding what is right and what is wrong," so is it necessary for an army to have rules of military conduct. In the Union these rules, based on English practice, were laid down in the Articles of War and in the Army Regulations. The Confederacy adopted the Union military code with only slight revision.

In both North and South the military code was administered by the President as Commander in Chief and the officers commissioned by his authority. Both the President and his military subordinates could mete out justice directly, within certain limitations, as a part of their command authority. But, except for minor infractions calling for light punishments, officers and soldiers charged with breaches of discipline usually were tried before military courts or courts-martial.

Courts-martial were of two principal types: general and special. Special courts-martial, convened on the authority of commanders of garrisons, regiments, and comparable organizations, were designed for the trial of lesser offenses. They consisted of three officers, and their jurisdiction was limited to enlisted men and to noncapital cases. They could not inflict fines exceeding a month's pay or impose prison or hard-labor sentences of more than thirty days.

General courts-martial consisted of from five to thirteen officers of rank superior to the accused. They were convened by commanders of armies or departments and, on the Federal side after December, 1861, by commanders of divisions and detached brigades. Their jurisdiction extended to all ranks and all types of cases, including capital offenses.

The North's judicial system included military commissions—comparable in authority and procedure to general courts-martial—whose function was to administer justice in areas where civilian agencies were inoperative. The jurisdiction of these bodies embraced both the armed forces and civilians. Most of the soldiers tried by military commissions were charged with crimes against noncombatants.

Confederate authorities made no use of military commissions. But inability of courts-martial to handle the great volume of business referred to them and the enormous demands which they made on officers needed for troop duty caused the Southern congress in September, 1862, to inaugurate a system of permanent military courts. The new plan as ultimately developed provided for the establishment of a court of three judges with the rank and pay of cavalry colonels and a judge advocate with the rank and pay of a cavalry captain for each state, military department, army corps, and cavalry division. Jurisdiction of these courts, which eventually aggregated twelve, extended to all offenses cognizable under the rules, articles, and customs of war, and to all ranks up to brigadier general. The judges, some of whom were former congressmen and disabled generals, were a very able group. The permanent courts eventually tried as many cases as general courts-martial. They undoubtedly brought a great improvement in the administration of military justice within the Confederacy.

Most Federals and Confederates were products of a new nation dedicated to the ideal that one man was as good as another. As civilians they had been accustomed to a considerable degree of individual freedom. Hence, it is not surprising that breaches of discipline were numerous and varied.

One of the most common offenses was absence without leave. Unauthorized departures from camp were especially frequent when soldiers were stationed near their homes or in the vicinity of large cities. Indulgent officers often winked at their men "taking a French," as the practice of running the guard was commonly called; indeed, one captain when asked by a soldier for permission to go to town, replied that he could not grant it but suggested that the applicant slip out on his own authority. But, regardless of the attitude of their commanders, soldiers found ways of "flanking the guards" and stealing at least a few hours of freedom. One ruse was to don disreputable attire, tuck a bundle of clothes under the arm, and head leisurely toward a creek as if on a washing expedition; then, when at a safe distance from camp, to change quickly into the garments taken along as laundry and make a beeline for town. Unless the absentee returned before the next roll call he was almost certain to be caught, though sometimes a comrade could cover up by answering for him or giving a trumped-up excuse for his not being present.

Brief absences usually drew only light punishment and sometimes none at all. When unauthorized leaves extended over a period of several days, severe penalties were sometimes imposed. But for this offense, as for all others, the punishments varied greatly with the circumstances. The character of the responsible commander was perhaps the most important consideration. Some officers were consistently strict; others were lenient; and still others were harsh or easy, depending on their peace of mind or the state of their digestion.

Soldiers, then as now, became experts at estimating the possibilities of detection and the severity of punishment in the event they were caught. The following statement, written by a Northerner to his sweetheart, might well have been written by almost any participant in any war: "The Col. here is mean he wont let the boys . . . have any passes. I take

General Marsena R. Patrick (Provost Marshal) and Staff, Culpeper, Virginia, November, 1863

a French pass once in a while but haft to look out for the petrolls. . . . Frank Hungerfox has just got back from . . . a french furlow and has got to go on extra duty for three days. I guess that I Shal go home on one if they get off as easy as that."

Drunkenness and brawling—the latter usually inspired by the former—vied with unauthorized leave for top place among camp offenses. Many unit commanders took no notice of moderate drinking during leisure hours. Indeed, a considerable number of them encouraged it by example and by serving liquor to soldiers on special occasions. George F. West, a Maryland private, tells in his diary of a "vocal serenade" which he and his comrades gave to General Beauregard on December 17, 1861, at Centerville, Virginia:

9. P.M. The singers all formed into line & we proceeded to his headquarters. We sang one of our old familiar songs when one of his aids politely invited us in & treated us to a stiff glass of old Rye, The General himself drinking with us. After we had drank . . . General Whiting advanced & gave us a short speech. . . . After he concluded he introduced General Beauregard, whereupon we gave 3 cheers & a tiger, which rent the air, with a deafning yell. The General spoke a few words of congratulation & thanks. . . . After he had concluded, we were again invited in & partook of another glass, Generals Beauregard, Jos. E. Johnston, G. W. Smith, J. E. B. Stewart and Whiting joining. Capt. Wm. A. Murray having charge of us, he proposed the health of the various generals, which was drank with a bumper. . . . [After midnight] we went to our separate tents to sleep away the excitement which was great.*

But most drinking sessions did not end so quietly as the one reported by West. A typical consequence of a whisky spree was described by Lieutenant Charles Johnson in a letter that he wrote to his wife on December 9, 1861, shortly after his regiment, the Eleventh Louisiana, arrived in Columbus, Kentucky:

Friday I was on duty as "Captain of the Guard". At night nearly the whole Regiment was drunk and I had my hands full keeping quiet and order in camp—with twelve drunken Irishmen in the Guard House and the rest of the camp in a high way. . . . Just about dark while I was at the Guard House . . . a drunken officer . . . commenced shooting at one of his men who was attempting to chastise him.

In later letters Johnson reported other drunken mêlées, which he attributed largely to the example set by the colonel, "who cannot get along without the stimulant." On March 30, 1862, he wrote from Corinth: Our entire Regiment has been drunk three or four days consecutively."

Brawls and drunkenness occurred most frequently on holidays and after visits of the paymaster. Private Charles F. West wrote from a Virginia camp on December 18, 1861:

Our Regiment are now paid off . . . [I am on guard and] I expect I will have some trouble . . . though our colonel, a very strict man, has put on 15 new guard to keep the men from purchasing liquor. . . . 11:30 P.M. Fight, fight, is heard all over our camp. . . . one sentinell on post No. 16 has been calling for the corporeal of the guard for the last 10 minutes. The corporeal goes to find out what is the matter & returns with 3 beastly drunken men cursing and swearing with eyes black and bloody noses. . . . all night the poor corporeal worried to death, by running from one post to another to bring in the respectable gentelmen, some so beastly intoxicated that the very ground which they tread flies up & bumps them . . . during my two hours of duty 78 persons were brought in by the various sentinels on the charge of too much friendship with

* The West diary is in the Maryland Historical Society, Baltimore. I am indebted to Charles A. Porter Hopkins for calling it to my attention.

"Bacchus." 1:20 [A.M.] A row now commences, the officer of the day bawls out, Turn out the guard & in a few minutes our Col. Stewart comes rushing out of his tent & goes in with a will, to tying, bucking & gaging the noisy ones. I'm sorry to say our corporeal . . . received a blow that split his left ear open.

In view of the regularity with which payday in both armies produced pandemonium and filled guardhouses, it is not surprising to find in a Union soldier's diary the entry: "On Guard today, have to be damed strict since they have been paid off; wish they knew enough to behave themselves."

Sometimes drunken free-for-alls resulted in fatalities. In a fight which broke out at Grand Junction, Tennessee, among two Irish companies en route from Louisiana to Virginia in August, 1861, eight men were killed "and a good many wounded."

Some units were much more susceptible to fighting sprees than others. Regiments causing the most trouble were those coming from the slum and waterfront areas of the large cities. But when liquor was obtainable drink-inspired disorderliness was deplorably common in nearly all organizations. In February, 1862, General George B. McClellan stated: "Drunkenness is the cause of by far the greater part of the disorders which are examined by the courts-martial."

Of course, fighting was not always provoked by liquor; and many encounters involved only a few persons. Army life compelled close association of uncongenial individuals, and this produced frictions and resentments which occasionally ripened into physical conflict. Again, teasing and banter would sometimes be carried to a point that caused tempers to flare and fists to fly. A Texas soldier wrote to his wife that he had just witnessed a fight between two comrades, "but they have made it up now and nobody hurt but a little scratch on one's countenance." He added that "the boys fall out and pass a few licks occasionally but they are sure to put them under guard for it." Squabbles such as those described by this soldier were quickly forgotten, but individual encounters sometimes caused serious injuries. A Mississippi lieutenant noted in his diary on December 25, 1863: "Parmenter & Barnhill . . . had a fight in which the latter had his nose bit off." One of Hooker's soldiers wrote from eastern Tennessee in March, 1864, that two of his comrades had recently clashed over a prostitute and that one of them had been killed.

Another common offense was theft. Stealing ranged in scope and character from individual soldiers lifting trifles from comrades, sutlers, commissaries, and civilians to highway robbery by roving bands and wholesale pillage of communities by regiments and brigades. One brazen instance of theft occurred at Castle Thunder, in Richmond, when a preacher who went there to minister to imprisoned Confederates had his pockets "denuded of their contents while he was supplicating the throne of Grace in behalf of the inmates." A comparable case was that of a group of Federals who stole the lumber that a soldier-minister had collected at great pain to build seats in a chapel for their use. In an outburst of righteous indignation the victim wrote: "I could not believe men could be found mean Enoughf to Do [such a thing]. Such men ain't fit for Dog feed."

As might be expected theft and pillage were more common among troops serving in enemy country than among those stationed in friendly localities. "Men who at home had a reputation for honesty and uprightness will steal everything that comes their way," wrote a Wisconsin captain from Arkansas in January, 1864, and his statement is borne out by an abundance of evidence, including the boasts of the thieves themselves. "We steal every

Provost Marshals of the 3rd Army Corps, December, 1863

thing that we Can get hold of—Money and cattel Sheep hogs and Salt," wrote a Hoosier to his mother from Oxford, Mississippi, in December, 1862.

Theft was practiced on people of all castes and conditions. Northern rogues ransacked Negro cabins and despoiled the occupants of their meager personal possessions. An Indiana surgeon stationed in Virginia wrote to his wife in December, 1864: "We have so many villains in our Army that rob & steal & commit outrages, take *Jewelry* from Lady's fingers —destroy everything in the house—& take the last mouthfuls of eatables on the premises even tho a half a dozen crying children stand by."

Federal soldiers marching through Kentucky in the fall of 1862 "Stole and carried off thirty stands of bees and Stole the honey" of a farmer who at the time was standing by the roadside serving water to the comrades of the thieves. An Illinois captain stated in his diary that "a Golden Christ was stolen by some of our thieves" from a church in Columbia,

Execution of Five Deserters Belonging to the 5th Corps. The Procession

South Carolina, and added the comment: "This army has done some awful stealing. . . . Everything imaginable is found in the wagons." A Massachusetts private wrote to his wife that some of his comrades robbed the graves of civilians buried before the war. "I am sick of soldiering," he added, "it is a lawless life; some of the men seem to fear neither God nor man."

Looting sometimes had its ludicrous aspects. An Iowa captain told of a Federal appropriating a hearse in Van Buren, Arkansas—"the only one in the city—which he loaded with an assortment of goods consisting of ladies bonnets, parasols, umbrellas, straw hats, calico and sugar, and confiscated a full-blooded donkey to draw the load."

Some Federal expeditions were orgies of plunder, especially Grant's invasion of northern Mississippi in 1862, Sherman's Meridian foray early in 1864, his march through Georgia and the Carolinas during the last year of the war, and Sheridan's Valley campaign of

1864. Most of the vandalism committed by the invading forces was the work of stragglers and "bummers" who formed only a small percentage of the army, and was perpetrated in violation of orders. Respectable men deplored the thievery, and high-ranking officers tried to prevent it, but the hoodlums would not be restrained. The excesses of the criminal element and the reaction of their honorable comrades may be illustrated by the comments of an Illinois captain who participated in Grant's northern Mississippi campaign of December, 1862, and a Wisconsin corporal who marched with Sherman to the sea.

The captain wrote from Waterford, Mississippi, on December 12, 1862:

Rebels, though they are, 'tis shocking and enough to make one's blood boil to see the manner in which some of our folks have treated them. Trunks have been knocked to pieces with muskets when the women stood by, offering the keys, bureau drawers drawn out, the contents turned on the floor, and the drawer thrown through the window, bed clothing and ladies' clothing carried off and all manner of deviltry imaginable perpetrated. Of course the scoundrels who do this kind of work would be severely punished if caught, but the latter is almost impossible. Most of the mischief is done by the advance of the army, though, God knows, the infantry is bad enough. The d——d thieves even steal from the negroes. . . . The army is becoming awfully depraved. How the civilized home folks will ever be able to live with them after the war, is, I think, something of a question.

The corporal wrote from Savannah on December 14, 1864:

The cruelties practiced on the campaign towards citizens have been enough to blast a more sacred cause than ours. We hardly deserve success. It is not that indiscriminate destruction of property is *ordered*—quite the contrary. A guard is placed at every house we pass with orders to admit no soldier, but he only remains while his division is passing—then come the trains accompanied by a thousand "bummers"—stragglers under nobody's charge—and they ransack the houses, taking every knife and fork, spoon, or any thing else they take a fancy to, break open trunks and bureaus, taking women or children's clothing, or tearing them to pieces trampling upon them &c. besides taking everything eatable that can be found.

Federals committed far more thievery against civilians than did Confederates. But the explanation lies in the fact that Federals for the most part served in enemy country and had better opportunities for plunder. True, Confederates did far less pillaging in Pennsylvania than did Federals in Georgia, but the objectives of the two campaigns were vastly different; Confederates were in enemy territory only a short while and they were on the move most of the time. Even so, diaries and letters written by participants in the expedition indicate that Lee's men succeeded in taking a considerable toll from Pennsylvania orchards and chicken roosts. A Georgian who boasted of going within seventy-five miles of Philadelphia wrote to his homefolk shortly after returning to Virginia: "We all had a fine time . . . we made milk and butter and chickens and eggs get up and dust. We lived on the best the[re] was in the State."

The conduct of some Confederate units operating in border areas suggests that if the North instead of the South had been the invaded land, Confederates would have gone down in history as the greater pillagers. The surgeon of an Arkansas regiment wrote to his brother from New Madrid, Missouri, in March, 1862: "The houses have been entered by the [Confederate] souldiers and everything that they could take with them they have carried away and what they did not want they wantonly destroyed. I have seen pianoes

. . . defaced . . . the strings cut out, the keys scattered and the legs off. . . . I have seen them take the finest of ladies' wearing apparel, with costly bonnets, and putting them on parade about with them, and in the end destroy them. This I have seen our soldiers do to those who have ever been *our friends,* surely an enemy could not have done worse." Similar depredations were reported in April, 1864, by a Montgomery newspaper correspondent attached to the Confederate "Army of Western Virginia":

Our troops are often guilty of outrages for which no punishment could be too severe. These things are usually kept concealed. . . . Forage trains, wagoners and wagon masters, with a few exceptions, are little better than gangs of rogues, who go about seeking what they can plunder. . . . No man's hen roost or smoke house is safe from these plunderers. . . . General John C. Vaughan's brigade passed through a portion of North Carolina while I was out there. I have been with many armies and seen many acts of outrage and depredation, but "General Varn's men" as they call themselves, are a disgrace to our cause. They stroll through the country, steal horses, rob hen roosts, break into houses, insult women and frighten children. . . . His brigade has made more enemies in the South in North Carolina than the Yankees have since the war began.

The greatest thievery on both sides was committed by detached cavalry commands. But most units, whatever their branch or assignment, had a considerable element who, given the opportunity, would steal—from friend or foe, present or absent, living or dead. After the battle of Fredericksburg, a New York sergeant wrote to his homefolk that he was going to send his money home before the next fight, because he had observed that the killed and wounded who lay on the battlefield frequently had their pockets turned inside out. "It is hard talk," he added, "but it is So; it is done on both sides." And his charge is substantiated by much other evidence.

Still another offense common among Federals and Confederates was insubordination. In its more serious forms this offense consisted of personal assaults on officers, and courts-martial records reveal many instances of soldiers attacking their superiors with fists, clubs, stones, muskets, and various other instruments. Some officers were killed in these encounters, and a few were probably shot down in battle by aggrieved men of their commands. Certainly a number of soldiers on both sides avowed to "get even" with hated superiors on the field of combat, and it seems reasonable to assume that at least some of them carried out the threat.

In the overwhelming majority of instances, insubordination was confined to disrespectful language. "Back talk," like other forms of insubordination, was usually associated with excessive drinking. Private G. B. Drew of Debray's Texas cavalry got drunk and told his lieutenant: "If you will take that Bar off your coat I'll be damned if I don't whip the xxx out of you." In this instance the court recorder deliberately omitted a vulgar term, but in most cases the barracks language used by the offenders was entered without any emendation into the proceedings.

Sleeping on sentry duty was fairly common among raw recruits, but rarely occurred after they became experienced. Every major battle yielded a sizable crop of skulkers and cowards. Cases of rape, murder, treason, and mutiny were occasionally brought before the courts, but by far the most frequent of serious offenses was desertion. Chronologically, desertion followed the same general pattern in both North and South, the rate being lowest in 1861 and highest during the last year of conflict. But the factors influencing the over-all trend differed in some particulars. The relative rarity of desertion in 1861 was due to

General Patrick's Punishment for Gamblers

176

the martial fervor and the expectancy of quick victory which then pervaded both sections; and the frequency of the offense in 1864–1865 was attributable in large measure to accumulated war weariness. But Confederates were influenced to leave the service during the latter part of the conflict by the increasing hardship of their families and the ever diminishing prospect of victory. These factors generally were not operative among Federals—though there can be no doubt that the despondency which engulfed the North in the dismal winter of 1862–1863 caused many desertions. But the high rate of desertion from the Union forces in the war's concluding year was due largely to a flooding of the camps with men whose major concern was the collection of the munificent bounties offered to recruits and who departed in droves at the first opportunity. Some men, known as bounty jumpers, made a profitable business of enlisting and reenlisting repeatedly under different names. The champion deserter by his own admission jumped bounty thirty-two times before finally being sent to the Albany penitentiary.

Deserters aggregated about 200,000 Federals and about 100,000 Confederates. If to these figures there be added absentees without leave, "hospital rats," and men at home with false certificates of disability, the totals become scandalously large. Compilations from the Northern side show that on January 1, 1865, absentees, authorized and unauthorized, totaled 338,536 as against 620,924 present for duty. Figures of about the same date for the Confederate forces list 198,494 officers and men absent as against only 160,198 present. In both cases the majority had no valid reason for being absent. What General Henry W. Halleck stated with reference to the Union forces in November, 1862, was applicable to both sides at any time of the war: "Absenteeism is one of the most serious evils in all our armies."

Punishments were considerably more varied than offenses. Unit commanders on their own authority meted out a vast assortment of penalties, known as company punishments, for minor breaches of discipline. More serious offenses normally were referred to special courts-martial; and the gravest infractions were tried by general courts-martial, military commissions and, in the Confederacy, by the permanent military courts. Punishments were supposed to correspond in a general way to this disciplinary hierarchy, with unit commanders dispensing the lightest penalties, general courts-martial assessing the heaviest ones, and special courts-martial meting out a type of intermediate severity. But in actual practice there were many deviations. Unit commanders occasionally inflicted on their men exceedingly severe punishments specifically prohibited by army regulations. "Drumhead" courts—groups hastily assembled to render summary judgment under "emergency conditions," thus in effect giving a semblance of legality to extreme punishment by high-ranking commanders—sometimes sent men to their death, without any opportunity for appeal or review of their case, within hours of their arrest. And in rare instances, regimental officers ordered soldiers to be shot without any form of trial.

On August 30, 1862, Lieutenant Colonel H. Robinson, in compliance with a directive from Major General Nathaniel P. Banks, Commanding General of the Department of the Gulf, ordered the consolidation of the remnants of the Second Rhode Island Cavalry with the First Louisiana Cavalry. The Rhode Island regiment protested the merger, and when ordered to move over to the ranks of the assembled Louisiana unit some of the men refused to obey. Robinson repeated the order, and when those holding out still refused to obey, Robinson selected two privates whom he considered the ringleaders and within a half-hour had them shot before the whole command. In battle, during a violent mutiny, and under other circumstances where imminent mortal peril is involved, a commander holds the power of life and death over his men. But no such situation confronted Colonel Robinson. He undoubtedly could have had the offending men seized and held in confinement until their case, admittedly serious, was referred to high authority. But he assumed the power of executing them on the spot, and he not only was upheld by a military commission which investigated the incident but also was commended for the "prompt and efficient manner" in which he had suppressed the disorder.

Both the punishment inflicted by Colonel Robinson and the method by which it was ordered were exceptional. Perhaps the most frequent of all punishments was confinement in the guardhouse. This institution usually was not a house at all but a tent, an open pen or stockade, or simply a marked-off area watched over by one or more armed guards. Confinement ranged in duration from a few hours to a month, depending on the seriousness of the offense; sometimes prisoners were limited to bread-and-water rations during all or a part of their incarceration.

Another common punishment was the wearing of a ball and chain. The ball was normally a cannon ball, weighing from six to thirty-two pounds, and it was attached to the leg by a chain two to six feet long. Culprits were required to walk about the camp, for varying periods, dragging the shackles behind them. A similar penalty was the carrying of a weighty object of some sort—a log balanced on the shoulder, a bag of dirt or bricks tied to the back, or a rock or cannon ball held in the hands—for repeated stints of one to four hours interspersed by brief periods of rest. This could be a very painful punishment. A Texan told of a comrade who, for firing his gun in camp, had to carry a heavy log for three hours: "The first hour he done well, the second hour he was walking slow and looking serious and changing the stick from right to left and from left to right and calling for the time of day, and long before the third hour was out he was begging for mercy."

A corrective frequently applied by unit commanders was to force men to parade the company streets wearing large placards specifying their offense, such as "Coward," "Thief," or "I stole a skillet." A Union cavalryman had to walk up and down the parade ground carrying on his back a saddle that he had stolen. A Confederate who appropriated a citizen's pig had to wear the porker's skin around his neck in the presence of his comrades; and another Southerner who got the jitters while on picket and shot a dog had to lug the dead animal about the camp at double quick pace. A Confederate found guilty of selling whisky in camp was placarded with the notice "Ten Cents a Glass," and ridden about the camp on a rail, with three bottles dangling from his feet.

Many petty misdoers were subjected to the humiliation of "wearing the barrel shirt." The barrel was fitted by cutting a hole in the bottom, so that it could be slipped over the wearer's head, and by making openings in each side through which to pass his arms. Usually a sign indicating the misdeed was attached to the outside of the "shirt."

Other lesser punishments were assignment to extra guard duty—though some officers condemned this practice on the ground that it tended to degrade a responsible function intimately associated with soldierly honor—digging ditches, grubbing stumps, riding the wooden horse—a horizontal pole held aloft by two upright beams—standing on some conspicuous pedestal, such as a barrel, stump, or box, and cleaning the company grounds.

A penalty frequently imposed for insubordination was bucking and gagging. This consisted of placing the offender in a sitting position, tying his hands together and slipping them over his knees, inserting a pole or musket beneath the knees and over the arms and tying a stick or bayonet in the mouth with a string. When prolonged for several hours, as frequently was the case, this was a terrible punishment. An officer who witnessed the bucking and gagging of a Federal artilleryman at Memphis in 1864 wrote afterward to his wife: "[after] 4 hours he was sobbing and crying as if suffering greatly. When untied he was not able to walk. . . . He was *carried* to his quarters."

Even more inhuman was the punishment, frequently meted out for "back talk," of tying men up by their wrists or thumbs with a rope thrown over a limb. Sometimes the victims were allowed to rest their full weight on their feet, but the general practice was to tighten the rope until only the toes touched the ground, thus placing great strain on the wrists or thumbs and causing the cord to cut into the flesh. Little wonder that men subjected to this torture after a while groaned and screamed in agony and that comrades, incensed by the brutality, angrily demanded their release and even cut them loose, sometimes at the risk of being subjected to the same punishment themselves.

A cruel punishment used in the artillery was to strap a culprit, with arms and legs ex-

Drunken Soldiers Tied Up for Fighting and Other Unruly Conduct

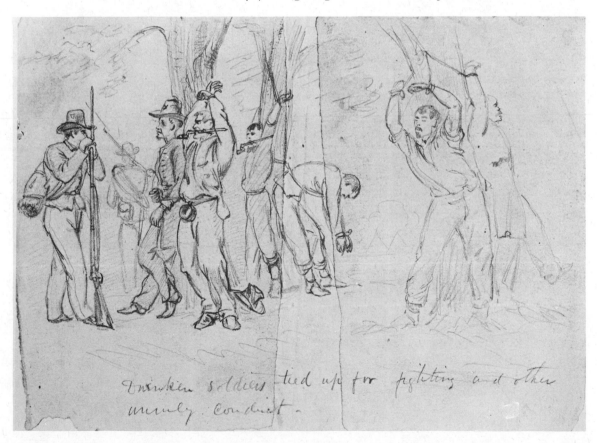

First Military Execution in Washington: Hanging a Private for Shooting His Superior Officer

tended in spread-eagle fashion, to the spare wheel carried on the rear of the caisson. If the vehicle remained stationary, and if the victim lay with his head at the top of the wheel for no more than an hour or two, the discomfort might be relatively mild. But if the wheel was given a half-turn so as to place the prisoner in a horizontal position, the time extended to several hours, and the caisson driven over rough roads, as was sometimes the case, excruciating pain would ensue.

The Federal and Confederate congresses by Acts passed respectively in August, 1861, and in April, 1862, prohibited the flogging of soldiers. But the injunction was sometimes ignored. A general court-martial found Brigadier General John McNeil guilty of having two Union privates publicly whipped, each with thirty-nine lashes, in Barry County, Missouri, on November 8, 1864. And on March 29, 1863, a North Carolina soldier wrote to his father: "well pappy those men that you saw whiped heare . . . are dead and the Col. [who had them flogged] are under arrest."

Both North and South accepted branding as a legal punishment throughout the war, and courts-martial records show that it was widely used. The brand was usually the first letter of the offense committed—"D" for desertion, "C" for cowardice, "T" for thievery, and "W" for worthlessness—and it was either stamped on with indelible ink or burned into the skin with a red-hot iron. The usual place of application was the hip, hand, forehead, or cheek.

Deserters, cowards, and other serious offenders sometimes were required as a part of their punishment to have half or all of their head shaved. To this and other penalties occasionally was added the provision that the victims be dishonorably discharged, stripped of their buttons and insignia, and drummed out of camp. Drumming out was done to the tune of "The Rogue's March"—Confederates sometimes substituted "Yankee Doodle"—with soldiers in front and behind carrying arms reversed—in the presence of the regiment, brigade, or division to which the culprit belonged.

Another punishment frequently prescribed for serious offenses was imprisonment. Terms varied from a few years to life, and the place of confinement was usually a penitentiary, or a military prison like the Federal "Rip-Raps" near Norfolk or the Dry Tortugas off the coast of Florida.

A few capital offenders were hanged, but most soldiers who paid the death penalty were shot by firing squads. The shooting of soldiers was an awful spectacle, described in gruesome detail by many soldiers in their letters and reminiscences. The horror of these affairs was frequently enhanced by the clumsiness which required as many as three rounds of firing before the victims were finally put out of their misery. A concise description of the preliminaries, as well as a vivid portrayal of how the climax might be terribly mismanaged, is contained in Lieutenant Francis Galwey's account of the shooting of two Union deserters on September 18, 1863, near Culpeper, Virginia:

The Division formed three sides of a hollow square. The open side was a hill. At the foot of this two graves had been dug. Shortly after we had completed our formation, the sad tones of a dead march smote our ears and a funeral procession entered through an opening at the other end of the square. It consisted of the Division Provost Guard . . . under the Division Provost-Marshal, with a band, and two ambulances, each carrying a deserter sitting on his coffin, securely guarded, and a Chaplain endeavoring to prepare his unfortunate client for death. The procession halted at the graves and the dead march ceased. The prisoners descended from the ambulances and the coffins being placed, each in front of a grave, the poor devils were made to sit upon them after being pinioned and blind folded. Before being blind folded however, the sentence of the General Court Martial was read to them, and was also read at the head of each regiment in the division. Then, after, prayers by the Chaplains, and when all was ready, two firing parties from the Provost Guard took position, one in front of each victim, and at a command from the Provost Marshal, pulled triggers. One of the two was slightly wounded and fell over, struggling on his coffin; the other was not hit at all, but with desperate energy broke his pinions and snatched the handkerchief from his eyes.

A murmur of mingled pity and disgust ran through the Division. Most of the pieces had only *snapped caps.* Here was either wanton carelessness in the Provost Guard, or a providential interposition to save the lives of the men. General French the Commander of the Division was in a rage at the awkwardness of the Provost Marshal and his men. The firing parties changed their pieces for others and fired again, the unhit man again being blindfolded and pinioned, but with no other result, that we could see, than again to wound the already wounded man, and to drive the other into a paroxysm of fear and nervousness without even hitting him! An audible groan passed now through the Division.

The left hand squad fired again and killed the wounded Deserter for he fell back upon his coffin and never stirred again. But the right handed squad only *wounded* the unhit man, who continued to struggle to free himself from his pinions.

The guns had evidently been prepared the evening before and had been dampened by the rain which fell during the night. The Provost Marshal now brought up his men one by one, and made them pull trigger with the muzzle almost touching the poor devil's head! But strange to relate, they only snapped caps the victim shivering visibly each time. At last the Provost Marshal himself, drawing his revolver, placed the muzzle against the man's head and discharged all the barrels into it! This finished him. He fell over onto his coffin and became motionless.

General French rode up and we could plainly see was indignant at the butchery, for that was butchery. We returned to our camps right afterwards.

The number of men who forfeited their lives for offenses committed during the Civil War cannot be ascertained. A nearly complete list of executions on the Federal side aggregate 267, with breakdown as follows:

Desertion	141
Murder (including two instances of murder and desertion)	72
Rape (including two instances of rape and some other crime)	23
Mutiny	20
Spying	3
Theft or pillage	4
Other (multiple offenses)	4
Total	267

The same general pattern would probably apply to the Confederate forces.

Sleeping on sentry does not appear in the list of offenses for which common soldiers were executed. It was a capital offense; officers did a great deal of talking about its seriousness; and a considerable number of men adjudged guilty of dozing at their posts were sentenced to be shot. But the records do not show a single instance of a Civil War soldier paying the death penalty for sleeping on sentry.

The manner in which Union and Confederate authorities dealt with sleeping on sentry points up one of the most notable characteristics of Civil War discipline; namely, its capriciousness. In many instances soldiers found guilty of the most serious offenses received sentences so light as to make mockery of military justice; at the other extreme were

182

Handcuffs

numerous cases of inhuman punishment for trifling breaches of discipline. A Confederate court-martial in 1861 sentenced Private A. C. Everett for sleeping at his post near the enemy to three days in the guardhouse on bread-and-water ration and justified its leniency on the ground that on the night he was found asleep Everett had partaken of "an extraordinary quantity of liquor to which he was not accustomed," and that during eight days of confinement preceding his trial he had manifested a penitent attitude. Even more amazing was the case of Joshua C. Ward, a Pennsylvania soldier whom a court in February, 1862, found not guilty even though it had been shown during the trial that "when visited by the relief, he was lying on the ground fast asleep; that he was shaken and shouted to before he could be roused [and] . . . arose in great wrath against those who had waked him . . . [cursing them] for waking and kicking him." General McClellan in reviewing Ward's case gave the court a verbal lashing. But the records reveal many comparable instances in both armies.

Six Confederates who deserted from the Army of Tennessee late in 1862 apparently got off with "a little fatherly advice" from their commanding general, and a Mississippi district judge stated in 1864 that he knew many soldiers "now in desertion for the fourth, fifth and sixth times who have never been punished." After a court in the Army of the Potomac in September, 1861, gave to five serious offenders trivial punishments, including forfeiture of one month's pay, for desertion, McClellan was moved to state: "Military crimes to which the articles of war annex the heaviest penalties are treated as if they were the most venial misdemeanors."

The opposite extreme of dealing with offenders was exemplified by the case of a Union soldier described by a member of the court as "a poor blockhead" who in the fall of 1862, for five days' absence without leave, was given three years at hard labor without pay.

As a general rule punishments became more severe and discipline more effective as the war progressed, though many striking exceptions were noted even near the end of the conflict. The progressive improvement was due in large measure to a gradual weeding out of inferior officers and to the increasing habituation of the men to strict discipline.

From the beginning to the end of the conflict punishment was marked by many inequities. Among these, none was more flagrant than the gross discrimination with which the dispensers of justice treated their fellow officers. One notable example of this evil, which in varying degrees was common to both armies, was a court-martial of McClellan's command which sentenced a private to wear a ball and chain for thirty days for being under the influence of liquor when called as a witness; and which punished not at all an officer who appeared in the same condition. Another example is afforded by contrasting sentences handed down in 1864 by two different courts-martial of the Army of the Potomac: one prescribed the death penalty for a soldier who deserted his post in battle; the other simply cashiered an officer convicted of the identical offense.

The Rogue's March, Morris Island, South Carolina, July, 1863

The inscription on the board reads: "THIEF this man Benj. Dutcher 55th Mass. stole money from a wounded friend."

185

Morals and Religion

eight

Sunday Morning Inspection, Cumberland Landing, Virginia, May, 1862

"There is the most wickedness in the army, nothing but a stedy stream of vulgar & Profane language, I have heard it till I am worn out," wrote a Connecticut private from a camp near Fredericksburg on January 8, 1863. Ten months later one of Longstreet's men stationed near Chattanooga wrote to his sister: "It is very distressing to hear how God's name is profaned in the Army."

An abundance of evidence substantiates the testimony of these two soldiers about the talk heard in Civil War camps. Profanity was repeatedly condemned by chaplains as the most prevalent evil with which they had to contend. They denounced it regularly in their sermons and passed out innumerable tracts on the subject. Military authorities issued general orders such as that promulgated by General O. O. Howard on March 5, 1865:

The attention of officers and soldiers of this army is called to the gross and criminal practice of profane swearing which prevails and is increasing amongst us, so much so that every sense of good principle and good taste is outraged. Have we forgotten that God is our kind Father and that He is helping us? Every insult to Him is a scourge to ourselves and invites disaster to our noble cause.

But these and all other attempts to restrict profane and obscene language were of no avail. One of the most convincing proofs of their futility is the fact of their increasing repetition and emphasis. A Confederate chaplain depicted a situation applicable to both armies when he wrote near the end of the war: "The air, indeed, is so filled with profanity that it seems to swear without a tongue. The sound of blasphemy everywhere; disturbs my rest; pollutes my dreams; desecrates my devotions." This minister stated that he had "heard more cursing and swearing in twenty-four hours" in camp "than in all my life before," and expressed the fear "that I shall learn the loathsome practice myself." A South Carolina soldier said of his comrades: "Suffering and horror . . . tend only to harden their stony hearts. They march into the very jaws of death profaning His name—even when the missiles of death are flying thick and fast around them, they curse and swear."

In the autumn of 1861, a North Carolina chaplain wrote from the Virginia front: "Young men that never drank at home are using spirits freely in camp." His statement was undoubtedly true, and what he said of Southerners was equally applicable to Federals. Removal of home restraints, boredom, loneliness, anxiety about the future, and the example of bibulous comrades all combined to make excessive drinking notoriously common among both officers and men. "There are other great evils in the army," wrote a Maine journalist from Maryland Heights in June, 1863, "but none is to be compared with drinking. It is the key to every other vice."

Overindulgence was more common among Federals than among Confederates since the men in blue had more money with which to buy liquor and were issued whisky rations more frequently than their opponents. The liquor ration was too small to intoxicate, but letters and diaries show that drinkers regularly wheedled, bought, or traded sufficient quantities from teetotaler comrades to get pleasantly tight if not uproariously drunk.

Trips to town afforded opportunity for slaking thirsts which many soldiers utilized to the fullest extent. Much ingenuity was displayed in devising ways to obtain liquor in camp. Feminine visitors bootlegged it beneath their expansive hoopskirts. Peddlers secreted bottles in watermelons, fish, cakes, bread, and other wares hawked through company streets. Soldiers bribed camp guards or outwitted them by hiding forbidden beverages under their hats, in their boots, or in innocent-looking packages. One Federal, according to a comrade, "smuggled a quantity of liquor out of Alexandria by putting his flasks in a child's coffin and then with a sad face such as a bereaved father might be expected to wear, he bore his spirits, by no means departed, across the river and into camp."

Once soldiers got the liquor to their quarters, they managed to make it last for several days, by burying it beneath the floor and drawing it out through a hidden tube or straw.

A favorite ruse was to submerge a keg of whisky in a spring or creek just outside the camp, fit it with a hose which extended above the surface into a clump of weeds and then, on the pretext of taking a draught of fresh water, "tank up" on the contents of the keg.

Every conceivable device was employed to tap the supply of whisky kept by surgeons and commissaries. A group of Federals assigned to guard commissary stores removed the bung of a liquor barrel, inserted a musket barrel into the hole, and surreptitiously took a swig each time they made their rounds until all of them were intoxicated. They had to wear a barrel shirt for ten days, but this must have seemed light punishment for such a rare and satisfying treat. Other soldiers crawled up under supply houses, bored holes through the floor and into the bottoms of whisky barrels and drew off the contents. Members of an Illinois regiment stationed near Paducah early in the war slipped out of camp one night to a barricaded distillery, climbed up on the roof, and let one of their number down the smokestack with a rope. He filled a demijohn with bourbon, and after he and his jug were pulled up the chimney the whole party got gloriously drunk.

In quality intoxicants ranged from fine to foul. Both extremes were reflected to some extent in the nicknames which consumers applied to camp potables. These included: "Oil of Gladness," "Rock Me to Sleep, Mother," "Rifle Knock Knee," "Bust-Skull," "Tanglefoot," "Nockum Stiff," and "Old Red Eye." A Union soldier who marched through central Kentucky in the spring of 1863 wrote enthusiastically to his homefolk: "This is the place where the regular *pure* Bourbon is made and truly it *is splendid,* much better than I ever tasted before. . . . I had not been able to get warm for a number of days, and I don't believe a little whiskey will hurt anyone who has to sleep on the damp ground." But few soldiers, North or South, were able to enjoy the products of Bourbon County's renowned distilleries. Most of them had to be content with general issue "commissary" or worse. A Hoosier lieutenant stated that the ingredients of "commissary" were: "tan-bark juice, tar-water, turpentine, brown sugar, lamp-oil and alcohol." A Richmond newspaper reported that the stuff dispensed at high prices to thirsty Confederates who visited the capital was "about thirty per cent alcohol and the rest is made with water, vitriol and coloring matter."

The effects of liquor varied as much as the quality. A Union private who recorded his reactions in his diary while still under the influence stated: "Mrs. Turner brought down some Ale have had a damn good time since it has been here been tight as a pup all the time." This soldier seems to have spent his spree in inoffensive festivity. But many if not most inebriates became disorderly, and whenever a company or regiment obtained access to a large amount of "How Come You So," fighting was almost certain to follow, and this in turn often led to insubordination, destruction of property, and sometimes to manslaughter and other serious crimes. A Massachusetts colonel stated in 1864: "Two-thirds of the troubles which have arisen in our regiment since its formation can be traced to intoxicating liquor alone." And he reflected a sentiment held by many unit commanders in both armies.

Theft and pillage occurred with deplorable frequency on both sides, but these have already been discussed. Another evil, less common but still not so rare as published records would indicate, was association with prostitutes. In the 1860's when a soldier mentioned the subject of sex in a letter or a diary the reference usually was deleted before the document was published. But random references in unpublished correspondence, and materials gleaned from medical records, inspection reports, and courts-martial proceedings indicate that the conduct of Federals and Confederates with respect to women of ill repute was neither better nor worse than that of participants in other wars.

Most of the allusions to amorous exploits found in soldier correspondence appeared in letters written by young men to equally uninhibited contemporaries at home. A Confederate lieutenant boasted to one of his friends: "John you ought to have been with me Christmas. I together with several other officers went over to Petersburg. . . . Staid two days and nights. . . . I tell you it is a heap better than sleeping with a man." Another Confederate wrote to the same correspondent: "John . . . I have not got but three tast[e]s since I have been in Va. and that I run up with[in] the great city of Petersburg, and I got that from two fine looking women I tell you the three goes cost me but eleven dollars." In September, 1864, a private in Lee's army wrote from near Petersburg: "You can get a plenty of Grous here but you will get wounded nine times out of ten, not with the clap but with something worse."

In similar vein, in February, 1865, a New Hampshire private wrote from Savannah, Georgia: "[T]here is the most hoars here that ever I saw in my life boath black and white. I thought that Washington had enough but this beats that."

Chaplain Gordon Winslow, 5th New York Infantry, U.S.A.

Prostitutes sometimes came into camp disguised as peddlers and washerwomen. An Alabamian wrote to his wife from Mobile in May, 1862: "One of these mean women came into our camp the other night on pretense of selling cakes. It was ascertained afterwards that 7 of our boys and 31 Georgians scr—d her last night. . . . Don't you think she ought to be satisfied?" A Georgian stationed near Savannah informed his spouse in July, 1862: "they are several women in camps at this time, go on like the men, sleepe in the tents like another boy croud in where they are thre or four and sleepe sum of the Boys naked sum one way and sum another."

Occasionally prostitutes donned uniforms and passed as soldiers to ply their trade in camp; and in some instances their true identity was concealed so long as to suggest collusion with officers and men. A Richmond newspaper on October 31, 1864, announced arrival in the Confederate capital of Mary and Mollie Bell alias Tom Parker and Bob Morgan. "They were dressed in Confederate uniforms," according to the reporter, "and were sent to this city from Southwestern Virginia where they had been in the service during the past two years." They were tried on the charge of "aiding in the demoralization of General Early's veterans" and given a prison sentence. A Philadelphian told in his diary of a woman of easy virtue who had apparently posed as a soldier being drummed out of Camp Washington at Easton, Pennsylvania, in June, 1861, to the tune of the Rogue's March.

Negro women who flocked to the Federal lines to claim the freedom associated with "the Day of Jubilo" sometimes became the victims of soldier lust. A Maine soldier stationed near Washington wrote a friend that he and his comrades had nothing to amuse themselves with "but little nigger wenches," and an Ohio sergeant who marched with Sherman noted in his diary on December 5, 1864, that four of his company "put themselves to the debasing test of copulation with Martha Boo of Madison (colored)." One of the reasons that Sherman, Grant, and other Federal commanders opposed Negroes remaining about their camps was concern for the health and morals of soldiers and freedmen.

Prostitutes set up shop wherever large numbers of troops congregated. New Orleans, Mobile, Savannah, Vicksburg, Memphis, Cairo, Louisville, Cincinnati, Chattanooga, Nashville, Jacksonville, Raleigh, Petersburg, Portsmouth, Norfolk, Chicago, and New York all had their share of bawdyhouses catering specially to soldiers. Private George H. Cadman of the Thirty-ninth Ohio Regiment wrote from Memphis in May, 1863: "Women and whiskey are plentiful here, and the men had been so long debarred from both that it did not take them long to raise hell generally. Never did I see such a scene before . . . and I hope to God I never may again." Private J. M. McNeill of the Seventy-eighth Illinois Regiment, who previously had served on a guard detail charged with keeping Buell's men out of Louisville whorehouses, wrote in his diary at Nashville on June 9, 1863: "On our way we passed through one of those dens of vice common to all large citys, but this having more than its due proportion . . . a section wholly given to houses of ill fame. We never saw anything to compare with this. Louisville does not compare at all."

Other sources substantiate McNeill's impressions of Nashville. Newspapers repeatedly deplored the nightly orgies that took place in "Slabtown," "Smoky Row," and other underworld sections of the Tennessee capital. In January, 1865, a Federal surgeon reported that registered prostitutes in Nashville aggregated 393; and there must have been many others who failed to make themselves known to the provost marshal.

The principal centers of vice seem to have been the two national capitals. Prostitutes swarmed into Richmond in the early summer of 1861 and there they remained throughout the war, walking the streets, frequenting places of amusement, exposing themselves in the doors and windows of bawdyhouses and otherwise making themselves known to prospective customers. And soldiers undoubtedly comprised the major portion of their clientele.

Conditions in Washington were even worse. An official count made in 1862 revealed 450 houses of prostitution and in 1863 a newspaper survey indicated that 7,500 women of the streets were doing business in the national Capital. Franc B. Wilkie, the war correspondent, compared the city to Sodom and Gomorrah. "The majority of women on the streets were openly disreputable," he stated, "and, in fine, every possible form of human vice had flowed into the capital and made of it a national catch-basin of indescribable foulness." Little wonder that a Union private after visiting Washington in 1863 reported to a friend at home that he saw "a Plenty whores."

Soldiers who patronized prostitutes almost inevitably became the victims of venereal infection. A medical statistician concluded that during the first year of conflict one out of every twelve soldiers on the Union side had venereal disease and that for the entire war the annual venereal rate was 82 cases per thousand soldiers. Venereal cases reported to Union medical authorities from May 1, 1861, to June 30, 1866, totaled 197,036 of which 102,893 were gonorrhea, and 79,589 syphilis. Fatalities from these diseases aggregated 168. These figures are low, for all cases were not reported and records on colored troops were not available for the period prior to July 1, 1864.

Confederate statistics are too sparse and scattered to permit a comparison of Northern and Southern venereal rates. But in view of the fact that Confederate soldiers were not so well or so frequently paid and not so often stationed near cities as their opponents, it is reasonable to assume that they had less opportunity for lewd associations and hence were less frequently contaminated. But random health records preserved in the National Archives show that when circumstances were such as to encourage philandering, Southern regiments sometimes ran up shockingly high venereal rates. Monthly sick reports for the Tenth Alabama show that this unit, which arrived in Richmond early in the summer of 1861, had in July, out of a mean strength of 1,063, sixty-two new cases of gonorrhea and six of syphilis. Other rural regiments which early in the war moved from the Deep South to the Virginia capital had similar experiences. In July, 1861, the total for twelve regiments drawn from five states and having a mean strength of 11,452 was 204 new cases of gonorrhea and 44 of syphilis. In subsequent months the venereal rate of these regiments declined, owing probably to a tightening of discipline and transfer of the units from Richmond to the combat zone.

Venereal patients ordinarily were sent to general hospitals for treatment. Some hospitals maintained separate venereal wards, and in a few instances both Union and Confederate authorities established hospitals for the exclusive care of men afflicted with syphilis and gonorrhea. Confederate surgeons treated venereal diseases with mercury and with extracts obtained from the roots and berries of various plants, including poke, elder, sassafras, jessamine, and prickly ash. The *Richmond Medical Journal* credited Dr. H. Chalmer Miles with success in treating gonorrhea with purgatives and blisters. Another Southern practitioner, Dr. J. Jacobs, claimed that "silk weed root put in whiskey and drunk . . . [along with] pills of rosin from the pine tree, with very small pieces of blue vitriol . . . [will] cure obstinate cases of gonorrhea."

Union surgeons rarely employed herbal extracts in the treatment of venereal diseases. Remedies used in Federal hospitals included injections of sulfate of zinc, nitrate of silver, and sugar of lead, light diet and cauterization. There is a hopeful note in the report of

Chaplain Sullivan H. Weston, 7th New York State Militia

196

Surgeon Isaac F. Galloupe of the Seventeenth Massachusetts Regiment on February 20, 1863: "All cases thus treated recovered without secondary disease."

In January, 1864, one of Sherman's soldiers wrote to his parents: "I don't know what is going to become of me surrounded [as I am] by eavel doings." Four months later a private in Lee's army remarked to his wife: "A man certainly stands much more in kneed of religion in the Army than at Home."

Churches North and South, keenly aware of the needs expressed by these two soldiers, made a valiant effort to repel the forces of evil which besieged the camps of the contending armies. Methodists, Baptists, and Presbyterians excelled in numbers and were the most aggressively evangelistic, and these denominations took the lead in promoting religious activities among the soldiers. But Episcopalians, Lutherans, Catholics, Jews, and various other groups manifested great zeal in looking after the spiritual welfare of their military constituents.

The churches were represented in the armies by chaplains, and it was to these agents that soldiers normally looked for spiritual guidance. Chaplains were a recognized part of the old army organization, and in May, 1861, both Union and Confederate governments provided for their inclusion in the volunteer forces. Each regiment was authorized a chaplain, who officially was appointed by the President or War Department but in practice was selected by the unit. Confederate chaplains normally were elected by a vote of all the regiment; on the Union side they were chosen by field officers and company commanders.

The pay of Union chaplains was $100 a month; Confederate chaplains at first received $85 a month, but a Mississippi layman, vigorously arguing the injustice of allowing ministers who preached only on Sunday the same compensation as lieutenants who worked every day, succeeded in getting the stipend reduced to $50; in April, 1862, however, the amount was increased to $80.

Confederate chaplains were free to dress as they wished. A picture of Chaplain J. William Jones published in *Christ in the Camp* shows a gray uniform with black trimmings consisting of pants, vest, and long frock coat. Confederate chaplains of the Army of Tennessee in 1863 adopted as the badge of their office a golden Maltese cross worn on the collar; in the Army of Northern Virginia many chaplains used the letter "C" as their insignia. The Army Regulations specified for Federal chaplains a plain black uniform of frock coat, pantaloons, and a forage cap or black felt hat.

The status of chaplains was not clearly defined, and this caused them considerable difficulty. They were listed with staff officers on regimental rolls, usually just below the surgeons, but they were not accorded traditional grades and no provision was made for their promotion. In 1863 a chaplain assigned to a Union regiment registered a sentiment that must have been shared by many ministers in both armies when he complained that chaplains lacked authority to draw tents for worship, requisition supplies, or issue orders to the men "for anything connected with their religious or moral improvement." Instead, he stated, chaplains were entirely at the mercy of commanding officers, many of whom had little or no interest in religion.

Chaplains were known to soldiers of the sixties as "Holy Joes" and "Holy Johns," though some had nicknames that were more openly disparaging.

In quality chaplains ranged from very poor to very good. Most eminent ministers did not exchange the security of civilian positions for the hardships and uncertainties of military assignments. Clerics of this class usually preferred to restrict their army service to periodic visits or short-term missionary connections. Thus chaplaincies all too frequently were filled by mediocre or inferior ministers who had little interest in their work. An Englishman who fought for the Confederacy termed the initial crop of Southern chaplains "a race of loud-mouthed ranters . . . saddled on our regiments . . . offensively loquacious, upon every topic of life save men's salvation." A veteran of the Army of the Potomac stated that "at least seventy-five percent of the chaplains commissioned during the first year of the war were practically unfit for their work."

Hard campaigning and accumulated opposition eventually relieved the armies of many disreputable ministers, but a substantial number of incompetent men were able to hold on to their positions. On the whole the quality of Civil War chaplains was poor, though many notable exceptions were to be found on both sides. Some were deficient in education; others were lazy; still others had little or no real concern for the spiritual welfare of their charges. Some were cowards; others were knaves; and courts-martial records reveal a sprinkling of sots.

Their shortcomings are abundantly documented in soldiers' letters. During the Atlanta campaign a Confederate informed his wife: "The chaplains of our Brigade seem to have forsaken us altogether. They are back with the wagons lying around the cook places and quartermasters." About the same time one of Lee's soldiers noted in his diary: "It seems strange that having three chaplains in the brigade we cannot have services . . . but they are so careful of their precious bodies they can take none for our souls, which is their business." In his reminiscences Private Sam Watkins of Bragg's army gave a sarcastic account of a "brave chaplain" crying out as the fighting began at Chickamauga, "Remember boys that he who is killed will sup tonight in Paradise." This was too much for one soldier, who yelled back at the top of his voice: "Well, parson, you come along and take supper with us." Just then, as shells began to burst close by, the chaplain spurred his horse and headed for the rear. This brought from the ranks a chorus of shouts: "The parson isn't hungry and never eats supper."

Comments of Union soldiers were even more critical. A New York artilleryman wrote to his wife in 1863: "Our chaplain is a nuisance—without energy, attainments or talent, addicted to tippling and a lover of loose conversation—he has become a standing butt for the regiment. His mouth alone would turn a man's thoughts from religion. Lecherous, misshapen, tobacco-stained and breathing corruption. . . . It does make me outrageous to think that eight hundred men have to suffer to gratify that old shallow fool's loquacity." A Massachusetts infantryman wrote to his mother in 1862: "Our chaplain is good for nothing. Never has any services. Doesn't visit the men. . . . The boys never call him 'Chaplain' but 'Postmaster,' and say he makes an awful poor one too."

Both Confederates and Federals sometimes denounced the sermons to which they were subjected. A Union lieutenant told of a chaplain inflicting on his audience a sermon on infant baptism which was concluded by an eloquent appeal to mothers. "I'm sure that there wasn't a mother in the audience," observed the lieutenant, "and not more than two or three infants."

The chaplains occasionally succumbed to the common evil of appropriating private property. A journalist reported the case of a minister of Hooker's army taking a horse from a Virginia farmer. When ordered by his superior to return the mount, the preacher replied: "Why Jesus Christ when he was on earth took an ass to ride into Jerusalem." To which the officer retorted: "You are not Jesus Christ; that is not an ass; you are not on the way to Jerusalem, and the sooner you return that horse to his owner, the better it will be for you."

In happy contrast to the ranters and incompetents who brought themselves and their positions into disrepute were a large number of chaplains whose character and conduct merited the esteem and affection of both officers and soldiers. Such men preached often, conducted numerous informal services, gave individual counsel, comforted the sick, encouraged the downhearted, wrote letters for the illiterate, set good examples of conduct, and shared fully the hardships of those to whom they ministered. Far from seeking shelter when battle was imminent, they went forward with their regiments, blessed the men as they prepared for the charge, aided the wounded, performed last rites for the dead, and wrote messages of condolence to bereaved relatives.

The work of chaplains on the battlefields was sometimes so outstanding as to merit official notice. Confederate General William A. Quarles in reporting an engagement near Atlanta in 1864 stated: "Rev. J. H. McNeilly, chaplain of the Forty-ninth Tennessee Regiment . . . exhibited the qualities of the Christian soldier. Following the blood-stained path of his regiment, he was everywhere to be seen ministering to the physical and spiritual comfort of the dying and the wounded." Following the battle of Prairie Grove, an Illinois colonel reported that "Chaplain R. E. Guthrie proved himself to be a soldier in every sense of the word. . . . He was on the field throughout the whole engagement, encouraging the men on in their good work, calling on them to trust in God, do their duty, and fire low."

Chaplains were regarded as noncombatants, and most of them appear to have confined themselves to peaceful pursuits. But in the heat of battle some found Mars a more compelling master than Jehovah. At Shiloh, according to a newspaper report, Chaplain I. T. Tichenor, of the Seventeenth Alabama Regiment, "fought with the coolness and intrepidity of a veteran, killing with his rifle a colonel, a major and four privates." And in an action near Columbus, Kentucky, Parson Brady, another Confederate chaplain, was said to have shot two Yankees, slashed the throat of a third with his knife, and then rushed after the routed foe crying, "Go to hell, you damned sons of bitches."

During the siege of Vicksburg a Union chaplain noted in his diary that he had been out in the trenches popping away at the Confederates. "I got several shots," he reported, "five times I fired deliberately, each time at a head which was incautiously exposed, and once . . . at a man's arm." Brigadier General Giles A. Smith in his report of the Battle of Atlanta cited Chaplain R. B. Bennett, of the Thirty-second Ohio, who "carried his musket and fought all day in the ranks, which I learn is his custom on all such occasions. After becoming exhausted he employed Private Mitchell . . . to load for him, who was

Bishop Leonidas Polk (Episcopal Bishop of Louisiana). Killed at Pine Mountain, Georgia, June 14, 1864

killed by his side." Bennett fought for two days, "firing rapidly and cheering and encouraging the men" and then "busied himself relieving the wounded and bestowing religious consolation upon the dying." He was awarded "a gold medal of honor" for his gallantry during the fight.

Casualties were an inevitable consequence of such boldness. One Southerner, B. F. Ellison, chaplain of Madison's Regiment, was mortally wounded while fighting in the front rank at Monette's Ferry, and another, Father J. Emerson Blimeol, Catholic chaplain of a Kentucky regiment, was killed in the fighting near Atlanta and buried on the field of battle. Union casualty records list a total of eleven chaplains killed in action. Among these were Chaplain O. N. Benton of the Fifty-first New York regiment, killed at New Bern, North Carolina, "while nobly encouraging the men," and Chaplain Arthur B. Fuller, Sixteenth Massachusetts, killed at Fredericksburg, rifle in hand, while participating in a skirmish, and after having received official discharge from the service.

The attitude and example of commanding officers had a great influence on the work of the chaplains and the spiritual tone of their units. Among high-ranking Confederate leaders who actively supported religious activities were Robert E. Lee, E. Kirby Smith, Stonewall Jackson, Jeb Stuart, W. N. Pendleton, and Bishop General Leonidas Polk, who early in 1864 baptized J. B. Hood, Joseph E. Johnston, and William J. Hardee. Jefferson Davis became a communicant of the Episcopal Church during the war, and professions of faith were made by Generals Bragg, Ewell, Pender, Rhodes, Paxton, and R. H. Anderson.

Northern leaders who manifested exceptional interest in religious activities included William S. Rosecrans, a devout Catholic, and O. O. Howard. Both McClellan and Burnside while commanding the Army of the Potomac issued general orders urging attendance of divine services.

In both armies some of the generals and many lesser commanders preached occasionally to their men. Visiting ministers and representatives of the United States Christian Commission also led services from time to time. Eminent Southern divines were especially zealous in this work, and the eloquent sermons and compelling presence of such outstanding leaders as John A. Broadus, J. B. Jeter, J. B. McFerrin, Stephen Elliott, B. M. Palmer, J. C. Stiles, and J. N. Waddel did much to promote the cause of religion in Southern camps.

The character and frequency of religious exercises varied greatly with time and circumstances. The principal service of the week normally was held on Sunday afternoon so as not to interfere with the regular weekly inspection. This service usually consisted of a sermon, scripture reading, and songs. Texts frequently had a martial flavor, as indicated by these favorites: "Put on the whole armor of God," "Fight the good fight of faith," "Through God we shall do valiantly," and "If God be for us who can be against us?" Sermons for the most part were simple messages stressing the cardinal virtues, warning against the common evils of camp, proclaiming the redeeming power of divine grace, pointing up the uncertainty of life, or threatening sinners with eternal damnation. Chaplains on both sides made a special point of proclaiming the cause supported by their audiences as the cause of righteousness and hence destined eventually to triumph through God's aid. Defeats were interpreted as temporary setbacks resulting from sin, and if reverses continued over a long period, the extended tribulations and ultimate delivery of the children of Israel were cited as grounds for continuing faith.

Both North and South experienced occasional periods of intense religious activity. These seasons of revival usually were characterized by increased awareness of sin, frequent prayer and preaching services, fervid exhortations by ministers and laymen, earnest seeking of sinners for salvation, and numerous conversions to the cause of Christ. On the Union side, revivals were small-scale affairs rarely extending beyond the limits of a brigade. But, among Confederates, and especially during the last two years of the war, they spread rapidly from unit to unit until entire armies felt the tremendous force of their accumulated impact. On September 8, 1863, a private in Lee's army wrote to a friend in Georgia: "Such revivals as are now going on in the different Brigades as never has been the like before. Soldiers are being converted by the score. The weighty bark of the holy spirit is abroad among the soldiers . . . and it is a general thing in the army of Virginia." A soldier stationed at Minden, Louisiana, reported a similar movement in that area, and from a camp in northern Georgia one of Bragg's men wrote to his sister that "thousands have professed religion and the work is still going on."

Revivalism subsided when active campaigning was resumed in the spring of 1864, but in the following fall and winter a new awakening spread through the Confederate camps.

The question naturally arises: Why were revivals so much more common and far-reaching among Confederates than among Federals? The answer may be found in the following circumstances: The Southerners were a more homogeneous group, in birth, language, occupation, and general culture. Evangelical sects were relatively stronger in the South than in the North. Ministers generally had greater prestige in Southern than in Northern society. Southern leaders, and especially the military chiefs, were more active in promoting religious activities among the soldiers than were their counterparts in the North. A private wrote from a Virginia camp during a revival in the spring of 1863: "Gen. Jackson (God bless him) has given us the privilege to be exempt from Morning's Drill in order that we may attend preaching." And Jackson was only one among Southern generals who followed this practice and who encouraged the revivals with their presence and prayers. Southerners with their limited resources felt greater need of Divine assistance than did Northerners conscious of their enormous strength in men and materiel. This was especially true of the last two years of conflict, and in this connection it is interesting to note that the great army-wide revivals did not occur until after the catastrophic defeats at Gettysburg and Vicksburg. These irreparable losses impressed on Confederate believers the necessity of obtaining strength from a source above and beyond themselves if their cause was to triumph.

What of the influence of religion on morale? The religion to which most soldiers on both sides subscribed was very personal. Hence its effects varied from one individual to another. Some unit commanders expressed the opinion that the chaplains' emphasis on divine punishment unnerved men for combat. Others complained of the chaplains' reiterated pleas for supposedly penitent sinners confined in the guardhouse; but these were a very small minority of the officer corps. Religion unquestionably made army life more tolerable for many soldiers. The aid of religion in accepting the hardships and uncertainties of soldiering is suggested in the observation of a humble Confederate to his wife: "my life is in his hands and what is his will ought to be ourn."

A Confederate chaplain of the Roman Catholic faith wrote after extended service with combat troops: "I have learned by personal observation that no men fight more

Chaplain's Quarters, 1st Connecticut Heavy Artillery in Confederate Fort Darling on the James River, April, 1865

bravely than Catholics who approach the sacraments before the battle." Many Protestant chaplains expressed similar views, and there seems no reason to doubt that citizen soldiers steeped in American traditions of a century ago derived help from their religious faith as they submitted themselves to the terrible ordeal of musketry and cannon.

What of the effect of religion on morals? Analysis of the comments of chaplains, records of courts-martial and other sources bearing on this question leave the impression that the effects of revivals were usually of short duration and that for every individual who was thoroughly and permanently reformed by religious influences were to be found several who after a few weeks or a few months relapsed into their evil ways. Except for brief periods during and immediately following the great revivals of 1863 and 1864, swearing and gambling seem to have been just as prevalent among Confederates as among Federals; and if drinking and some other practices labeled as sins by the chaplains were less common among Southerners, the fact must be attributed to lack of opportunity. In both armies sin flourished to a far greater extent than righteousness. But sinners frequently were not so evil as they seemed. Oaths, for example, became so firmly established in camp parlance that their utterance was more a matter of thoughtless habit than of conscious blasphemy. And so it was with other evils. To a large extent "sins" were symbols of soldiering, worn like uniforms. Many men who swore, gambled, and caroused in camp became model citizens and pillars of the church when they returned to their homes. And finally, not to be overlooked were thousands like Private Orville C. Bumpass of the Eighth Mississippi Cavalry who on October 22, 1864, wrote to his wife: "*Uncontaminated* I left home & so I expect to return," and Private Henry Cady of the Fourteenth Wisconsin Infantry after whose death at Vicksburg in July, 1863, a comrade wrote: "[He] was universally acknowledged to be the best boy in the Comp'y; amid oaths and curses that would [have] shook any one who heard it for the first time, he was never known to use an oath; he also kept free from all camp vices . . . he was always . . . good, kind and accommodating."

Sunday Morning Mass in Camp of the 69th New York State Militia, July, 1861

The Sick and Wounded

nine

Company E, 9th Veteran Reserve Corps, Washington, D.C., April, 1865

"At the station according to the *Washington Evening Star* Grant found a company of the Invalid Corps on duty drawn up in line with arms presented. The general, obviously touched by the sight, passed through with his head uncovered."

The Veterans Reserve Corps, successor to the "Invalid Corps," was organized in 1864. It consisted of one engineer regiment and nine infantry regiments. The Veterans Reserve Corps was composed of wounded and disabled soldiers and sound soldiers whose three-year enlistment had expired but who did not want to reenlist for combat service.

nine

In August, 1862, a North Carolina soldier informed his homefolk that "these Big Battles is not as Bad as the fever." About a year later an Ohio private wrote to his parents that "there is more dies by sickness than gets killed." They were both right. The opposing forces lost far more men from sickness than from hostile bullets.

On the Union side, where health conditions were relatively good, of a total of 360,222 deaths, only 110,070 resulted from enemy fire; the other 250,152 were due mainly to disease. Records are too sparse to permit an accurate tabulation of Confederate losses. After a study of available materials on the subject, Professor James G. Randall seemed inclined to accept as the best estimate an aggregate of 258,000 Confederate deaths of which 94,000 were combat casualties and 164,000 the result of sickness, accident, and other causes not associated with battle. The figure of 94,000 appears to be a reasonable approximation of battle losses, but 164,000 is clearly an underestimation. The preponderance of evidence from the *Medical and Surgical History of the War of the Rebellion* and other pertinent sources shows that both the incidence and mortality of nearly all illnesses were greater among Confederates than among Federals. Trustworthy figures show that on the Union side, nearly two and a half times as many men died of disease as perished from combat. Joseph Jones, an eminent Georgia surgeon who after the war became an outstanding authority on Confederate medical history, wrote in 1870 that three-fourths of the deaths in the Southern armies resulted from illness. Certainly it is safe to conclude that on both sides in the war, between two and three men died from sickness for every one who perished through hostile action.

One of the most striking testimonials to the achievement of modern pathology is the remarkable reduction in the ratio of fatalities from disease. In World War II nearly three times as many American participants died of battle causes as from illness, the figures being respectively 293,986 and 113,842. Combat fatalities would have been much higher (for the tools of war have become increasingly destructive) in World War II had it not been for the miracles of modern surgery.

One of the saddest commentaries on the tragedy of the Civil War is that more Americans died in that terrible struggle than in all our other conflicts. American fatalities from all causes in the Civil War (accepting Randall's figure of 258,000 for the Confederacy) were about 618,000 and in all our other wars, from 1775 to the present, about 606,000.

The shocking prevalence and deadliness of sickness in Civil War armies is not difficult to explain. A fundamental reason was ignorance of the cause of disease. Bacteriology was an undeveloped science. Malaria and other illnesses were attributed to "miasms" from the swamps and noxious vapors floating through the air. Hence sanitation and other safeguards against the contraction and spread of infectious disease were woefully inadequate.

Another basic cause of the frequency and mortality of disease was the haphazardness of induction procedures. Thousands of men were accepted as soldiers who either were suffering from chronic maladies or who were in such poor physical condition that they were easy prey to camp epidemics.

A third contributing factor was diet. Camp fare was usually deficient in fruits and vegetables; especially so on the Confederate side. Vitamin pills and concentrated juices were, of course, unknown, and milk was rarely obtainable. Meat frequently was cooked in a sea of grease, and bread often was fried hardtack or flapjacks. Extras sold by sutlers and peddlers were restricted largely to pies and cakes—"pi-zan cakes," as one soldier put it.

Shelter and clothing were often insufficient to protect the soldiers from snow, rain, and cold. Confederates were more exposed to the elements than were their opponents, but men of both sides frequently were soaked with rain and chilled to the bone. Most soldiers thought nothing of lying down to sleep in soggy garments after a hard march. In winter, bivouacs resounded with irrepressible choruses of incessant coughers, foretelling the lengthening of lines at morning sick call and the crowding of hospitals with large increments of respiratory patients.

Filth was another factor. "Sanitation poor," "no sinks [latrines] provided," "sinks not used," were comments appearing with notable frequency in inspection reports. Men, accustomed at home to low standards and lax practices which characterized young America, were slow to change their ways when they entered the service. Most of them thought only of convenience when disposing of waste, and many manifested the same nonchalance in responding to the calls of nature. A Confederate noted in his diary on December 3, 1863: "On rolling up my bed this morning I found I had been lying in—I won't say what—something though that didn't smell like milk and peaches."

Refuse and offal lying about the camps attracted innumerable flies, that swarmed into tents at will, crawled over food, and spread germs far and near. "There are more flies here than I ever saw any where before," wrote an Alabamian to his wife in June, 1862; "sometimes I get vexed at them and commence Killing them but as I believe forty come to every one's funeral I have given it up as a bad job. . . . Everything that attracts them is perfectly black."

Sickness was spread by numerous other pests. During the spring and summer, clouds of mosquitoes descended on camps and bivouacs, tormenting the soldiers and giving thousands of them the dreaded "fever and shakes." A Tennessean who served at Vicksburg stated that the "gallinippers" were more annoying than Yankee shells. "They would either get up in the blanket with you," he declared, "or they would bite you through all the folds." Another Confederate stationed on the Mississippi River avowed that the mosquitoes formed into regiments for their nightly forays, and a third stated that they were so big that they were "almost able to shoulder a musket." An Ohio soldier wrote from Cairo, Illinois, in September, 1862, that the mosquitoes were "big enough to have feathers on their legs," and an Illinois sergeant declared that those encountered at Suffolk, Virginia, were so large that instead of humming they brayed like mules." Some Federals and a few Confederates carried mosquito nets to protect themselves, but the overwhelming majority had no protection other than that afforded by the smoke of their campfires.

Many men complained of fleas. A Texan wrote from Mobile in March, 1862: "I do not think we will ever have a fight here except with the fleas. I think that there are 50 on

Hospital Stewards of 2nd Division, 9th Army Corps, Petersburg, Virginia, August, 1864

Hospital Attendants Collecting the Wounded After the Battle of Hatcher's Run, October 27, 1864

my person at this time." A Mississippi artilleryman wrote from a Virginia camp in August, 1861: "The boys are well and quite busy *fighting fleas*. This troublesome *quadreped* exists here to such a numerous extent that it seems that they collect in companies at knight fall for the purpos of carrying us off . . . though like the Yankeys they are repulsed by desperate efforts & great patience. I think [my battery] . . . is blessed with an entire brigade." A Massachusetts captain wrote disgustedly from Louisiana in 1863: "I have just found out what it is that bites so hard. The whole ground is covered with fleas. So you see we are in sore trouble with poisonous animals in the water, fleas on the ground and mosquitoes in the air."

The pests which caused the most swearing and inspired the tallest tales were body lice, or graybacks. "We all scratch alike, Generals and privates," wrote an Ohio sergeant early in the war. "The lice have grown to be a perfect torture to us. . . . A funny fellow named Jack Shepard . . . amused himself stringing the vermin on a thread for a necklace." A

Pennsylvania private wrote to his brother on February 6, 1863, from near Fredericksburg:

[After Antietam] . . . I do not believe there was a man in our brigade, officer, private or nigger, but was lousy. . . . They grow to enormous size and are the most cunning and most impudent of all things that live. During the late snow storm the boys . . . made sleds of their jaw bones and slid down the bank of the railroad. . . . I woke up the other night and found a regiment of them going through the manual of arms on my back. . . . Any one of them can throw himself into a hollow square and bite at the four corners.

One of the reasons for the prevalence of lice was neglect of personal cleanliness. A Georgian wrote to his wife in 1864: "We have some very filthy men in this company. Some wear their clothes two months without ever stripping . . . and they carry a right smart of rebels [lice] with them." Among Confederates scarcity of soap was a deterrent to cleanliness, and on both sides long and strenuous campaigns made it difficult to take baths and wash clothes. Even so, the prevailing filth must be attributed in large measure to low standards and lack of concern.

A critical factor in sanitation was command. All too frequently company and regimental officers set very poor examples of personal cleanliness and were very lax in establishing and maintaining sanitary discipline. On October 2, 1862, General Robert E. Lee wrote to President Davis: "Our sick are very numerous. . . . Until the regimental officers can

Ambulance Section, 57th New York Volunteers

be made to appreciate the necessity of taking care of their men, keeping them under control . . . and enforcing cleanliness, etc., I fear the sanitary condition of the army will not improve." And an abundance of evidence indicates that little if any improvement occurred among either Confederates or their opponents after this letter was written.

One of the most striking manifestations of the pervasive ignorance and indifference about sanitation and health was the lack of any system of providing pure water for the soldiers. Troops stationed near rivers and creeks drank the water just as it came from the streams, however muddy, polluted, or malodorous it might be. A Union soldier wrote from a camp on the Virginia peninsula in July, 1862: "The water we are compelled to drink is of the most miserable quality. I have drank so many wiggle-tails and polly wogs that I can hear young Frogs croaking all the time." A correspondent of the Chicago *Tribune*, wrote from Grant's headquarters shortly after Shiloh that the Tennessee River water "smells so offensively that the men have to hold their noses while drinking it." When streams and natural springs were not accessible, water was obtained from cisterns, shallow wells, and stagnant ponds; and sometimes drainage from latrines flowed into these improvised sources. A South Carolina colonel whose regiment was stationed at Corinth in May, 1862, wrote: "There was a great scarcity of drinking water. I have often seen a hole about 6 ft. square, ten ft. deep dug and in one corner of the bottom a group of men crouched around a small hole, waiting for the water and when it did come up it had probably passed through a nearby sink." In view of these comments, it is not surprising that both armies stationed near Richmond and Corinth in the summer of 1862 experienced crippling epidemics.

The officers and men placed much of the blame for the persistency and deadliness of disease on the army doctors. "Of all the men now in our army I think that the Surgeons are the most unworthy of all the human famaly," wrote a Georgian to his wife. An ailing Louisiana soldier complained to his homefolk: "These damn quacks we have got for Drs. . . . are doing me more harm than good. They know nothing but calomel & Quinine."

Yankee comments were equally derogatory. A Union colonel requested removal of the regimental surgeon in February, 1862, because "he has proved himself to be perfectly incompetent . . . not only unskilled but unkind to all his patients . . . by his neglect and rudeness many have died." A Michigan soldier declared: "Many army doctors are quacks. I have made sickness in the army quite a study and it is my opinion that three-fourths of the deceased soldiers have died from mal-practice. A Massachusetts private complained that "there dam poison . . . kills half the men." Another wearer of the blue gave a reasonably accurate summary of enlisted attitudes on both sides when he stated: "If there are men in the army who are deserving of eternal punishment . . . I believe about half of the M.D.'s are."

Soldiers have always tended to be ungenerous to their surgeons, and those who wore the blue and the gray were no exception to the rule. But, with due allowance for bias, the quality and performance of Civil War doctors appear to have left much to be desired. Standards and procedures of selection were often faulty. Many surgeons and assistant surgeons of regiments were appointed by state governors, and all too frequently the prime consideration in their choice was politics or personal friendship. In his report of peninsula operations in 1862, Surgeon Charles S. Tripler, the Medical Director of McClellan's army, stated that during the first year of the war "all sorts of doctors—steam, eclectic, and even advertising quacks—were sometimes commissioned as medical officers . . . so far as the

Dr. William S. Parran, Barboursville Blues, C.S.A. Killed at Sharpsburg, Maryland, 1862

Surgeon Robert S. J. Peebles, C.S.A.

public notion . . . was concerned any one called 'Doctor' was competent to perform the duties of military surgeon." As late as December, 1863, the Medical Director of the Union Army of the Tennessee, Surgeon John Moore, reported that "in three of the Western States surgeons are admitted and assigned to regiments without any form of examination whatever." The situation was no better, and very likely not even as good, on the Confederate side.

Surgeons had ready access to the liquor dispensed for medical purposes, and many of them seem to have abused this privilege. Phoebe Yates Pember, a matron in Chimborazo Hospital in Richmond, Virginia, had the greatest difficulty in preventing diversion of the whisky from patients to doctors. General Lew Wallace's medical director reported after the capture of Fort Donelson: "Dr. Sexton, an efficient and skilled surgeon when sober, was so much under the influence of liquor for twenty-four hours as to be incapable of discharging the responsible duties of his office." Courts-martial proceedings and other official records show that both armies had a considerable number of surgeons possessed of the same weakness as Dr. Sexton. On October 30, 1862, Quartermaster General Meigs, wrote to an official of the Sanitary Commission: "Ask the Surgeon General how many surgeons he has dismissed for drinking to excess. How many surgeons, nurses and stewards have been guilty of stealing and drinking the liquors provided for the sick. He will tell you a story which will fill you with horror."

Only a small percentage of army doctors were sots, but the training and skill of many were so lamentably deficient that they would have been about as effective drunk as they were sober. A New York chaplain reported the case of a doctor dosing repeatedly for "bilious fever" a patient whom a post-mortem revealed to have been suffering from peritonitis. Major Abner R. Small of the Sixteenth Maine stated that in his regiment standard prescriptions handed out at sick call were Number 6, a blue pill; Number 9, quinine; and Number 11, vinum (wine or brandy). These, according to Small, were dispensed to the line of ailing men in a rotation which ignored completely their different symptoms.

William H. Taylor, a Confederate surgeon, testified to similar procedure in Southern camps. When the patients assembled at sick call, he made a rapid diagnosis, "usually by intuition," and treated them with whatever medicine he happened to have on hand. In one pocket he carried a mercurial preparation known as blue mass, in another a ball of opium. "All complainants were asked the same question: 'How are your bowels?' If they were open, I administered a plug of opium; if they were shut I gave a plug of blue mass."

It is not surprising that many men in both armies scorned the treatment dealt out by regimental surgeons. Many doctored themselves with herbs and nostrums sent from home. Others elected to take their chances without medication.

The majority of doctors on both sides were honorable men who did their best. Some of them were talented practitioners, ever alert to new and better techniques; and collectively they used their war experience to achieve notable advances in medical science, as is well shown by the remarkable collection of specimens at the Army Medical Museum in Washington and the mass of data compiled and analyzed in the monumental *Medical and Surgical History of the War of the Rebellion*. In evaluating their work, cognizance must be taken of the numerous and formidable difficulties with which they had to contend. On both sides the supply of trained physicians and surgeons fell far below the enormous demands created by the war. In an effort to supply a surgeon and assistant

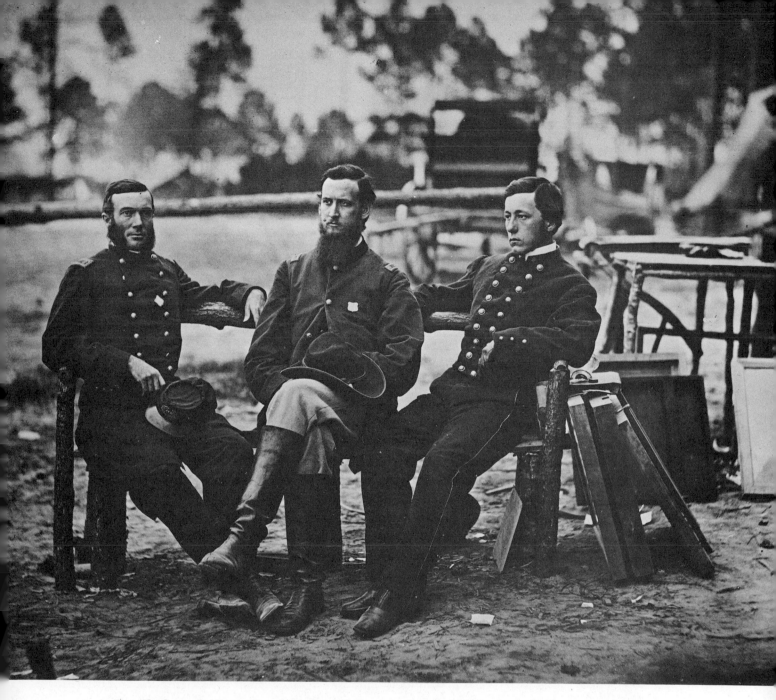

Dr. Blackwood (Center) and Medical Officers in Front of Petersburg, Virginia, 1864

surgeon for each regiment, and a minimum staff for hospitals and supervisory positions, doctors of inferior training had to be utilized. Even after resort to all possible expedients the medical corps was not large enough to cope with epidemics and the special situation created by a big battle. During such emergencies, overtaxed doctors worked until they were overcome with exhaustion. And it is not surprising that some of them took to the bottle in an effort to keep going a little longer.

On the Confederate side shortage of personnel, notably more serious than that experienced by the Federals, was complicated by inadequacy of transportation and chronic dearth of quinine, opiates, and other essential medicines. Ingenious utilization of native herbs and sundry other improvised remedies did much to compensate for drug deficiencies, but shortages persisted in varying degrees. Generally speaking, Southern doctors were always handicapped by lack of medical and surgical supplies, and the result was stupendous suffering on the part of their soldier-patients.

Cases of sickness reported on the Union side aggregated 6,029,564. Confederate figures are not available, but half this number would seem to be a reasonable estimate, thus bringing the total cases on both sides to something over 9,000,000.

Among camp illnesses, one of the first to strike in epidemic proportions was measles. This disease, like all others highly contagious in character, had a higher rate of incidence among Confederates than among Federals, and on the Northern side the rate was higher in the Western than in the Eastern armies. The reason was a greater admixture of rural men in the Southern and Western forces. Country soldiers derided their city-bred comrades for softness and frailty, but sick reports showed beyond question that men who came from the cities were healthier and often hardier than those from rural sections. The city dwellers had in most cases been exposed to measles and other epidemic diseases in childhood, when the effects were relatively mild. Among such men, previously unexposed because of their isolation, now congregated with thousands of others in the "camp-cities" that sprang up after Fort Sumter, these illnesses struck with devastating force. When men of city background became ill, they generally knew better how to take care of themselves than did their comrades from the country.

When Major General Mansfield Lovell in January, 1862, was urged by the Confederate War Department to send reinforcements to Albert Sidney Johnston, he replied: "I will . . . send to him the five Mississippi companies as soon as I can have them put through the measles, which they are now undergoing, one half of them now being sick." Other commanding generals, North and South, found that putting recruits through the measles was an essential part of the breaking-in process. From July 1 to September 30, 1861, one out of every seven men in the Army of Northern Virginia had measles. In one Confederate camp of 10,000 volunteers, 4,000 men were stricken. Among newly formed Union regiments, cases ranged in number from twenty to three hundred, and the principal factor in the prevalence of the malady, in these as in Confederate organizations, was the proportion of rural troops. Measles showed a preference for the winter. The highest peak of prevalency came in the first winter of the conflict, but the line on the frequency charts rose sharply during each succeeding winter and especially after large increments of recruits.

Measles alone was rarely fatal, but complications, resulting largely from patients getting up before they were fully recovered, led to thousands of deaths. The Tarheel who wrote

220

to his brother in July, 1861, "I had rather risk my life in a hard battle than with the measles in camp," would have found abundant support in the mortality records of both armies.

Another disease which prostrated thousands of soldiers, many of them several times, was malaria. One-fourth of all the sick cases reported on the Union side were malarial, and the average annual rate among Federals was 522 cases per thousand men. Confederate figures are too fragmentary to permit a meaningful estimate, but the disease was probably more prevalent among the Southerners than among their opponents. Soldiers on both sides commonly referred to malaria as "the ague" or "the shakes," and a common greeting in camp during the mosquito season was, "Have you had the shakes?" A North Carolina soldier wrote to his homefolk in the autumn of 1862 that he had just had a chill which "like to shook me clean out of the garrison."

Doctors on both sides treated malaria with quinine, though Confederates were compelled by shortage of the drug to use various substitutes, including "a compound tincture of dogwood, poplar and willow barks mixed with whiskey." Southern doctors on the suggestion of the eminent Confederate surgeon Joseph Jones—who knew of the prophylactic dosing of British seamen serving along the African coast—used quinine to a limited extent as a preventative.

Smallpox, pneumonia, tuberculosis, and yellow fever all took a considerable toll of lives in both armies. But the principal killers were typhoid and intestinal infections.

The incidence and mortality of typhoid cannot be definitely established, owing largely to confusion of terminology. "Camp fevers" or "continued fevers" which unquestionably were typhoid in most instances constituted one-fortieth of the total illness and caused one-fourth of all deaths from disease on the Union side. On the basis of fragmentary figures it appears that typhoid was similarly responsible for one out of every four deaths from disease among Confederates. In both armies the disease attained its peak in the autumn of 1861, after a tremendous influx of volunteers and before the soldiers had become accustomed to discipline. The general course of the frequency curve after November, 1861, was downward, with peaks occurring about the middle or close of each succeeding summer. But as cases declined in number they increased in virulence. On the Union side during the year ending June 30, 1862, 25.7 per cent of the typhoid cases among white troops proved fatal; for the year ending June 30, 1865, the figure was 59.5 per cent.

The ravages of typhoid were vividly reflected in the letters written from camp. An Illinois soldier wrote to his homefolk in November, 1861: "Tiford fever is Rageing here verry much their has been several deaths of it. . . . they hardly ever get over it." A Tarheel private informed his parents in August, 1862, that "T. G. Fremen is Ded and they is Several mor that is Dangerous with the fever they hev Been 11 Died with the fever in Co. A since we left kinston and 2 died that was wounded." Captain John W. De Forest wrote from Louisiana in the summer of 1863 that fever patients of the Twelfth Connecticut Regiment

cannot be kept in their wretched bunks, but stagger about jabbering and muttering insanities, till they lie down and die in their ragged, dirty uniforms. There are not enough well men to take care of them. . . . For swamp fever has turned our fine regiment into a sickly, dispirited, ·.n-disciplined wreck. . . . forty-two deaths in forty-two days; barely two hundred and twenty-five men left for duty; and most of those staggering skeletons covered with fever sores.

Surgeon Charles K. Irwin (Right), 72nd New York Infantry, and Assistant, September, 1863

Typhoid may have been the greatest killer, but diarrhea and dysentery between them (and army medical authorities lumped them together for statistical purposes) ran a close second. Doctors disagreed as to what diarrhea and dysentery were and what caused them. Much confusion resulted from the fact that looseness of the bowels is not really a "disease" but a symptom. But whatever their character or cause, the maladies classified by Civil War surgeons as diarrhea and dysentery were the most frequent of camp ailments. The soldier who went through the war without at least one siege of "flux," as intestinal infections were commonly known, was an oddity.

Statistics compiled by the Union Medical Department show an aggregate of 1,739,135 cases of diarrhea and dysentery, and an average annual rate of 711 cases per thousand men. Owing to the widespread reluctance of troops to consult army doctors, there must have been many thousands of unreported cases. Deaths on the Union side from diarrhea and dysentery are said to have totaled 57,265, but this, according to the *Medical and Surgical History*, "must be regarded as less than the actual mortality from these diseases." The incidence and mortality must have been even higher among Confederates, because of the South's relatively greater deficiencies in diet, medicine, and sanitary facilities. Certainly it seems safe to conclude that as many Civil War soldiers died of what they commonly called the sh—ts as were killed outright on the field of battle.

Soldier letters and diaries contain more references to bowel disorders than any other illness. A North Carolinian wrote to his wife: "I had a Sever attact of pukin & purgin saturday night but was abel for duty mondy morning." One of the most colorful comments was that of a Georgia soldier who wrote to his wife: "I have bin a little sick with diorah two or three days. . . . I eat too much eggs and poark it sowered my stomack and turn loose on me."

The most frequently used treatments for diarrhea and dysentery were alternate doses of laxative—usually salts or castor oil, if they were available—and opium. Quinine and calomel were prescribed by some doctors, but in May, 1863, Surgeon General Hammond stopped the issuance of calomel to Union doctors on the ground that they had used it to excess.

Confederate doctors frequently used derivatives of blackberry, willow, and sweetgum as astringents, and substituted various vegetable compounds for castor oil and salts.

Both Northern and Southern surgeons used remedies which today seem shocking and absurd. Men suffering from diarrhea sometimes had their intestines further irritated by heavy drafts of whisky and repeated doses of strong purgatives. A striking illustration of the ideas of the time is afforded by the recommendation of J. S. Newberry, one of the most eminent medical scholars of the sixties, after an inspection of Federal camps: "Bowel complaints might still be further reduced by the general adoption of the habit of wearing flannel body bandages or stomach belts, of which there is a large number at hand."

Treatment of the wounded was in many respects as archaic as that of the sick. John Will Dyer in *Reminiscences, Four Years in the Confederate Army* writes graphically of the plight of the men in the overcrowded, makeshift hospitals. "We had no anaesthetic dressing then, and all wounds were treated with the cold water treatment, which was to thickly bandage the wound and keep continually wet with cold water, till all signs of inflammation disappeared and the flesh began to show granulations. Then the water was discontinued, and dry bandages with salves and liniments substituted. Sometimes gangrene would develop, and unless quickly removed was sure death to the patient. Our method of re-

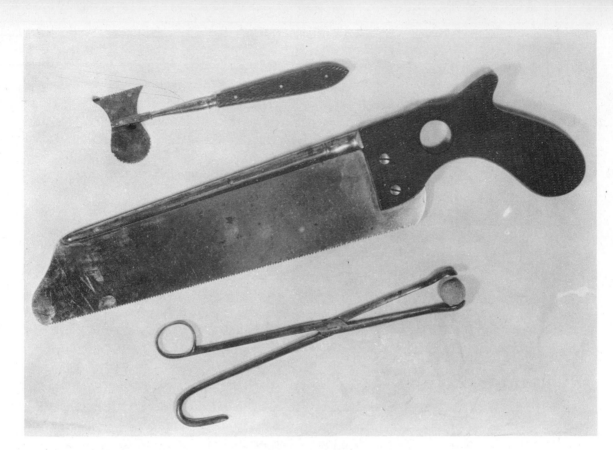

Surgeon's Instruments

Surgeon's Kit

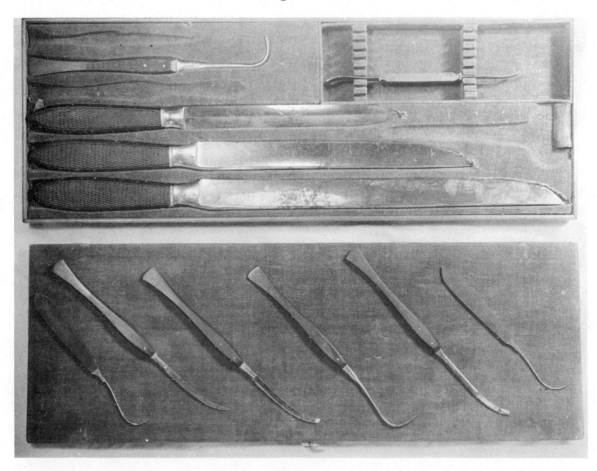

moving gangrene was to burn it out with nitric acid—aqua fortis. This was very severe and trying on the nerves of the nurse as well as the patient. When pouring the acid on the 'proud' flesh you would see smoke rise, the flesh sizzle and crisp up, and all this time the patient screaming in agony; it took a stout heart and steady nerve to apply it. I hope never to have to do it again."

W. W. Keen, a young Union surgeon, noting the chaos in caring for the wounded at First Manassas, was reminded of the days when "there was no King in Israel and every man did that which was right in his own eyes."

The aggregate of Federal wounded, according to Thomas L. Livermore, was 318,187. If the ratio of killed to wounded was the same on the Southern as on the Northern side, the total of Confederate wounded was about 271,000.

Ninety-four per cent of Civil War battle injuries were bullet wounds nearly all of which were caused by Minié balls. These soft lead missiles inflicted large and ragged wounds. They caused far greater injury than did the fast, clean, hard bullets used in later wars.

Fortunately for the victims, most soldiers who suffered wounds were shot in the arms or legs. According to the *Medical and Surgical History*, "of the wounds that came under treatment in the American Civil War . . . 10.77 per cent were injuries of the head, face and neck, 18.37 of the trunk, 35.71 of the upper extremities [shoulders, arms, hands] and 35.15 of the lower extremities [hips, legs, feet]." The most deadly wounds were those of the spine and abdomen; as a general rule "the ratio of fatality diminished with increased distance of the injury from the trunk." The percentage of fatality of various type wounds was: spine, 55.5; abdomen, 48.7; pelvis, 29.7; head, 28.9; lower extremities, 13.8; upper extremities, 6.5.

The organization for handling the wounded (and sick) was essentially the same on both sides. At the top was the medical department headed by a surgeon general. At the outbreak of the war the Surgeon General of the United States was a penurious, precedent-ridden octogenarian named Thomas Lawson, but a revolt instigated by the United States Sanitary Commission led to the appointment in the spring of 1862 of dynamic young William A. Hammond. Hammond's promotion over the heads of the entire corps of regular army doctors aroused considerable enmity which his temperament and methods did little to assuage. The principal cause of his downfall, however, was his inability to get along with the strong-minded Secretary of War, Edwin M. Stanton, who replaced him in November, 1863, with Joseph K. Barnes. But the army continued to benefit from the reforms which Hammond had initiated. These included a system of medical inspection by a specially chosen group of officers, the setting up of trained ambulance corps in the field armies, and the erection of large pavilion-type general hospitals.

The first Confederate Surgeon General was David C. De Leon but in July, 1861, Samuel Preston Moore was placed in charge of the Medical Department in Richmond. He held the position until the end of the war, and despite deficiencies in tact and a tendency toward highhandedness, his administration was notably successful. Among his achievements were the organization in 1863 of the Association of Army and Navy Surgeons of the Confederate States, "the oldest American military medical society," and the sponsorship of important medical publications, including *A Manual of Military Surgery*. He also played a key role in establishing in the Confederacy pavilion-type hospitals similar to those developed by Hammond in the North.

Directly below the surgeon general were the medical directors of the field armies. These officers had great responsibility and prerogative; and the farther removed they were from the capital the greater was the latitude that they enjoyed. The outstanding army medical director on the Union side was Jonathan Letterman, who developed in the Army of the Potomac the ambulance corps advocated by Hammond and who inaugurated a system of division and evacuation hospitals "which remained the basic structure of military medical care through World War II." At Antietam, where the thirty-eight-year-old Letterman's ambulance corps had its first test, 12,000 wounded were removed from the battlefield within twenty-four hours.

The most distinguished field administrator in the Confederate medical service was Samuel H. Stout, who achieved his distinction as medical director of hospitals in the Army of Tennessee, a position to which he was appointed by Bragg in the autumn of 1862. The placing of hospitals under an administrator who reported directly to the army commander represented an important departure from the standard organization. Under Stout's able supervision this plan worked well, and it would have functioned better if he had received more support and encouragement from his superiors in Richmond. Stout designed a pavilion hospital which had more spacious bed arrangements and provided better ventilation than other structures of this same general type. He also organized hospitals in such a way as to facilitate change of location; and his "mobile hospitals," while not without their shortcomings, proved a boon during the Georgia campaign of 1864. Before the end of the year Stout's hospitals, some of which had moved several times, and which together had treated thousands of patients, were scattered throughout the Southeast.

Below the army medical directors were corps and division directors. Medical activities of the brigade were usually supervised by a brigade surgeon who sometimes was also the senior regimental surgeon. Below the brigade surgeons were the regimental surgeons who were aided by one or more assistant surgeons, and a corps of litter-bearers, drivers, and menials. A Federal law of July 2, 1862, increased Union regimental assistant surgeons to two, but repeated efforts of the Confederate Medical Department to obtain similar legislation proved unsuccessful.

The field-hospital system on both sides consisted of regimental, brigade, division, and corps hospitals, each headed by a senior surgeon or director. As the war progressed both Federals and Confederates tended to pool regimental staff and equipment by brigade and division and to use only the most talented surgeons for operations. On the Northern side, division hospitals within a corps often were clustered together. In the Army of the Potomac under Letterman, and in some instances in other armies North and South, intermediate hospitals were established at depots such as City Point and Corinth, to care for casualties brought in from field hospitals pending their evacuation to general hospitals located beyond the combat zone. Patients were usually transported to evacuation points by ambulance or wagon, and from there to general hospitals by boat or train. Early in the war, and to some extent thereafter in emergencies following bloody battles, patients were transported in freight cars, passenger coaches, and any sort of water conveyance, but eventually both sides developed hospital cars and boats fitted with bunks and other special equipment designed to promote the care and comfort of the wounded.

General hospitals were headed by superintendents, some of whom were under the jurisdiction of army or department commanders, while others reported directly to the surgeon general. These hospitals were divided into divisions and wards each supervised by a sur-

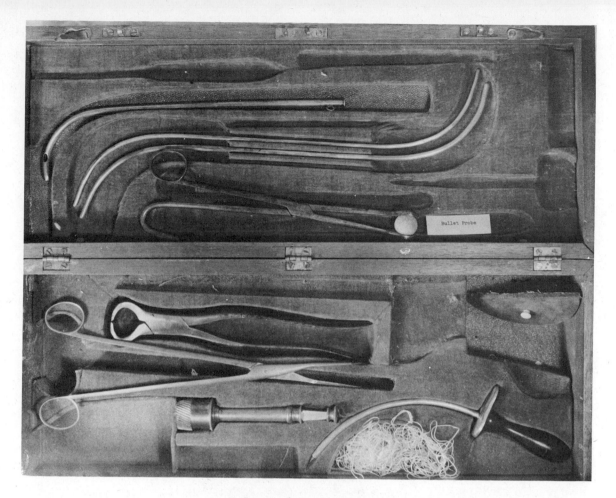

Surgeon's Instruments

geon or assistant surgeon. The staffs of some hospitals included matrons who supervised the feeding of patients and assisted in various administrative capacities. Nursing in most instances was done by men—who often were convalescent or invalid soldiers—but women served as nurses to a limited extent. Among the women who achieved distinction for their contributions in caring for Civil War wounded were Dorothea L. Dix, Clara Barton, "Mother" Bickerdyke, and Cornelia Hancock on the Union side; and Sally Tompkins—on whom President Davis conferred a captaincy and thus gave the distinction of being the only woman ever to hold a regular commission from the Confederate Government Juliet Hopkins, Ella Newsom, Emily Mason, Phoebe Pember, and Kate Cumming among Confederates. Louisa Alcott helped care for the Federal wounded in the Washington area, as did Walt Whitman. Hundreds of women, North and South, aided in providing bandages, food, and other necessities, and comforted the wounded by visits and personal ministrations. In the North various philanthropic agencies, and especially the United States Sanitary Commission, rendered valuable assistance to medical authorities. In the South state governments played a leading role in looking after the wounded. A Confederate law of September 27, 1862, provided that general hospitals be named and numbered by state and that, insofar as feasible, patients from the same state be hospitalized together.

Dr. Mary Walker, a Nurse Who Attended Wounded Under Fire on the Battlefield, and the Only Woman Awarded the Medal of Honor During the Civil War

Clara Barton, Civil War Nurse

Washington and Richmond became the principal hospital centers. The largest general hospital in the Confederacy was Chimborazo, superintended by the eminent surgeon James B. McCaw, which had 150 wards and during the war treated 17,000 wounded and 59,000 sick and was "the first military hospital in point of size . . . in the world." The next largest Civil War establishment was Lincoln Hospital in Washington which treated a total of 56,000 patients. Other very large general hospitals were Winder in Richmond and Armory Square in Washington.

In both armies the quartermaster department controlled the ambulances, boats, and trains which moved the wounded, and had considerable jurisdiction over personnel and supply. Poor coordination between military commanders, medical officers, and quartermaster authorities was perhaps the greatest and most persistent impediment to efficient care of the wounded.

Another great obstacle was a shortage of competent personnel. As previously noted, many doctors—and the aggregate, not counting surgeons, was about 11,000 on the Union side and something over 3,000 on the Confederate—were incompetent; and while the "butchery" of Civil War surgeons has probably been exaggerated, some of them were unquestionably "saw-happy," and a considerable number who ought never to have been entrusted with a cutting instrument, slashed and sawed away at will on patient after patient.

Stretcher-bearers commonly were musicians, or convalescent soldiers temporarily detailed. These comprised an "infirmary corps," numbering about twenty-five to thirty per regiment; in training and dependability they frequently were found wanting. Early in the war many ambulances were driven by civilians, and at the Second Battle of Bull Run nearly all of those on the Union side ran away, thus compelling Surgeon General Hammond to commandeer about two hundred hacks, omnibuses, and wagons on the streets of Washington and send them to remove the wounded. On the Confederate side ambulances were allotted on the basis of two four-wheeled and two two-wheeled vehicles per regiment, and on the Union side, one four-wheeled and five two-wheeled conveyances. Both types

Surgeon Robert C. Wood, U.S.A., Appointed to Sanitary Commission on June 9, 1861

left much to be desired, especially the two-wheelers, which were so extremely uncomfortable that most of them were eventually discarded. Many ambulances were so poorly constructed that they quickly broke down. Others were taken over for the conveyance of unit commanders and staff officers. As a result, many wounded were hauled from battle areas in cumbersome army wagons that bounced and jostled over the rough roads to the extreme discomfort of the occupants.

Letterman's reforms provided the Army of the Potomac with a trained ambulance corps made up of men permanently detailed for the duty; and his plan was eventually copied by the other Union commands. Similar improvements were made in handling Confederate casualties. But ambulances remained in short supply, and the flood of wounded produced by the big battles of May and June, 1864, overtaxed transportation, hospital, and all other medical facilities and led to great suffering.

On the Confederate side, suffering was enhanced by a continual shortage of medicines, especially chloroform (which was the most widely used anesthetic on both sides), surgical instruments, and all other supplies. Many Confederates underwent major surgery with liquor as their only palliative, and some had none at all.

The functioning of the medical organization under normal conditions was relatively simple. When the fighting began, the assistant surgeons, equipped with a small case of instruments and a stock of chloroform, morphine, liquor, tourniquets, bandages, splints, and other emergency supplies, moved forward with their stretcher-bearers to look after the casualties of their respective regiments. If circumstances permitted, they established primary stations just beyond musket range where first aid was administered to ambulatory patients and casualties borne in by the infirmary corps. But frequently they moved about from place to place to minister to the wounded.

Casualties were sent by litter or ambulance from forward areas back to field hospitals, which were tents or conveniently situated buildings previously prepared to receive the wounded. These hospitals, marked by distinctive flags, were normally located from one to two miles to the rear, so as to be beyond the range of artillery fire. Here the most urgent cases were sent as rapidly as possible to the operating table, which often were platforms improvised from doors. "Radical surgery"—which meant prompt removal of injured arms and legs—was a popular concept among Civil War surgeons, and the frequency of deadly infections gave support to their position. Hence field surgery consisted largely of amputation, and soldiers lying about on the ground, waiting their turn at the operating table, were treated to the gruesome spectacle of accumulating piles of severed arms and legs, not to mention the unpleasant sounds produced by the saw blades as they bit into bone and the agonized groans of the patients. Some soldiers refused to submit to the ordeal of amputation; and a few, including Rebel Private William A. Fletcher, saved their limbs, and perhaps their lives, by violently kicking with their good leg the doctor who insisted on relieving them of the injured one.

From field hospitals the wounded were moved by the most convenient means to evacuation hospitals located near wharves or railheads and to general hospitals situated in towns or cities. Houses, barns, churches, hotels, colleges, and warehouses frequently were converted into hospitals of one kind or another.

Sometimes patients were permitted to go home for a portion of their convalescence, though this was a privilege more frequently accorded to officers than to enlisted men.

Group of Nurses and Officers of United States Sanitary Commission at Fredericksburg, Virginia, May, 1864

Wounded Soldiers from the Wilderness, Fredericksburg, Virginia, May, 1864

234

Most patients returned to duty when they recovered, but some, known as "hospital rats," became so expert at malingering that they were able to extend their hospital sojourns to months and even years.

Generally speaking, the wounded fared worst during the first year and a half of the war when medical staffs were relatively sparse and inexperienced, organization undeveloped, and equipment inadequate. Suffering was especially great at Shiloh, where many of the wounded—who aggregated 16,000, about equally divided between North and South—lay on the field through one entire night of pelting rain, without shelter, food, water, or attendance of any kind. A large number of seriously injured Confederates were piled into wagons, many of which lacked springs, and jostled twenty miles to Corinth with the retreating army. There some of them were taken into the Tishomingo Hotel, while others lay about the railroad station—some for several days—until they could be moved to improvised hospitals at Oxford, Holly Springs, and Memphis. A Confederate nurse who attended the casualties at Corinth wrote in her diary: "The foul air from this mass of human beings at first made me giddy and sick. . . . We have to walk and when we give the men anything kneel in blood and water."

The Seven Days' fighting in Virginia, from June 25 to July 1, 1862, yielded an unprecedented flood of casualties, with Union wounded totaling 8,062 and Confederate 16,261. Richmond newspapers, for several days during and after the battles, pleaded with civilians to help evacuate and care for the suffering wounded. In response, hundreds of people from the capital and nearby towns thronged to the fighting zone with wagons, buggies, and carts, taking along food, water, bandages, and other supplies. Many of the wounded thus removed were taken to private homes, tobacco warehouses, stores and factories, but room could not be found for all, and hundreds lay on the streets and about the railroad stations for long periods awaiting transfer to hospitals farther removed. On July 3, 1862, two days after the close of the fighting, the Richmond *Dispatch* reported: "Vehicles of all descriptions were busily engaged the whole of yesterday in conveying from the battlefield the many wounded Confederate soldiers and . . . wounded Hessians [as the Federals were called]." On July 4th the same newspaper reported that the corpse of a soldier had lain for two days on a platform at a railroad station, "without the slightest effort being made for its interment." Despite the best efforts of citizens and the military, the wounded suffered unspeakable agonies and considered fortunate those of their comrades whom death quickly and mercifully released from torture.

On the Federal side even greater suffering was experienced. Many of the wounded left near the Chickahominy River and in White Oak Swamp as McClellan shifted his base to the James were unattended for several days. Some of those who were evacuated to White House and Harrison's Landing fared no better. When Sanitary Commission representatives arrived at the White House evacuation hospital after Seven Pines, they found a staff of five surgeons, one steward, and no nurses to look after the 4,500 wounded that were beginning to flow in from the battlefield. Many had received no medical care, and one group of three hundred casualties in crowded railroad cars had been without nourishment for three days.

Second Manassas was another time of exceptional suffering for Federal wounded, but Letterman's reforms led to improvement in subsequent engagements. The enormous toll of wounded at Gettysburg—17,684 Federals and 18,735 Confederates—hopelessly overtaxed

Union facilities, for the Northerners had to provide not only for their own casualties but also for many wounded Southerners. But the fate of those left on the field was infinitely better than that of seriously wounded Confederates who were hauled in heavy wagons over the long, rutted roads that led back to Virginia. Indeed, it is doubtful if any wounded in any war ever endured greater agony than that experienced by these unfortunates.

The heavy fighting of May 5 to June 3, 1864, brought another peak of suffering to the forces of both Grant—whose wounded during the period aggregated about 35,000—and Lee. Federal wounded, hauled over corduroy roads from Spotsylvania to Fredericksburg for shipment north, suffered such terrible pain that they begged drivers to shoot them and put them out of their misery. At the Wilderness, as in several other engagements, wounded lying helplessly on the field were roasted by fires that broke out in the underbrush.

As great as was the suffering resulting from Eastern fights, it was probably less than that produced by the big Western battles, for in the country beyond the Appalachians, remoteness from the centers of government and factors of distance complicated the problem of caring for the wounded. Difficulties experienced by Confederate medical authorities in this region were especially great, as Surgeon Samuel H. Stout repeatedly stated, owing to the vast areas over which operations extended, the inadequacy of the transportation system, and the inability—which Stout attributed in part to indifference—of the Confederate Medical Department to render needed assistance in personnel and supplies. At Chickamauga, for example, the single-track rail line that ran from Atlanta was so clogged that twenty carloads of wounded who had been hauled to the railhead over ten to thirty miles of rough mountain road were still waiting to be moved five days after the fighting had ended.

What was it like to be wounded in a Civil War battle? This question is so vividly answered in the diary of E. D. Patterson, a Tennessee Confederate shot twice at Frayser's Farm on June 30, 1862, that it is quoted here in full.

The first ball that struck me was so close that the musket's breath was hot in my face. I had my gun at my face in the act of shooting . . . and I fell forward across my gun, my left arm useless falling under me. The ball had struck me high up on my shoulder, and as I was leaning forward, and that arm extended at the time, the ball passed under my shoulder blade, and not much lower than it entered. I did not at the moment feel any pain, only a numbness all over the body. I felt as if someone had given me an awful jar, and fell as limber as a drunken man. I could not even tell where I was hit. But I was not left to pursue my meditations long, without interruption, for no sooner had I become conscious that I was a wounded soldier unable to get up without assistance, than I felt a decided assistance, for a ball fairly lifted me from the ground. Passing partly under me, it struck me in my left thigh, passing through that in a "slantingdicular" direction into my right, about half way between my knee and my body, and striking the bone ranged downward and lodged against my knee cap, I suppose from the looks of the wound since, that one ball did it all, though there may have been two. . . . I was afraid to move, even had I been able, for fear of increasing the flow of blood, and I felt that I had but little to spare. I thought that before daylight again dawned I would be in the presence of Him who made me, and for once in my life I looked death calmly in the face. I thought of more things in *one hour* than I could write down in a year. I thought of a home far away in the North-land [he was born in Ohio and his parents lived there]. . . . I wondered if my fate would ever be known to them. I had a horror of dying alone. . . . I was afraid that none of my regiment would ever find me, and that with the unknown dead, who lay scattered around me, I would be buried in one common ground, where no one but the Resurrection Angel would ever find me. To meet death

Tent Hospital Camp, Kendal Green, Washington, D.C.

under any circumstances must be terrible, but to die there, in the darkness of night, without being noticed by friend or foe—the thought was terrible. How I longed for day. Just that *some* one might see me die . . . and if ever an earnest prayer was sent heavenward by mortal, mine was one that night, but I had but little faith. I could not help thinking that had I escaped without being wounded, I would not have thought of praying. I would have been *glad*, and would have called that gratitude, and that would have been the extent of my devotional feelings. I found some comfort though, that my mother's prayers offered up to heaven long years ago, in my behalf would be answered. I had more faith in them than my own. . . . The loss of so much blood had made me cold. . . . I shook until I almost feared that I would shake in pieces. My teeth chattered until they were sore. . . . My limbs were as cold as ice and still I wanted water. . . . [A young Yankee soldier heard Patterson's cry for water and attended him all night. The next morning his cousin, Frank Patterson, surgeon of a Georgia regiment, found him and gave him a couple of draughts of brandy, took him to a house, and prepared to operate on his leg.] I wanted him to give me chloroform so that I would not suffer any more, but Frank said that it wasn't best and that it would soon be over and would not be very painful, so I must "grin and bear it." I did both. I watched him while he laid open the flesh and it reminded me of cutting fat pork, it cut so smooth and nice, and it hurt my wounds equally as bad as the place he was cutting. "Sympathy" he said. [Several weeks later Patterson had to submit to surgery a second time, which he described thus]. . . . Dr. Holloway opened my thigh. . . . My leg was as big as two ought to have been. While I was reasoning the case with him and asking him to give me chloroform, he pretended to be examining it, and the first thing I knew I had his knife in me and the operation performed "Before I could say Jack Robinson."

He survived.

237

*"Pass the Infantry
to the Front"*

ten

Waiting for Dawn

"Very early on the morning of the 21st, ranks were formed of unrested men: some had not slept at all, some had just begun to sleep, none had slept adequately. Before them was a march—and battle. Time was lost in forming units; time was lost in reporting to higher commanders that units were ready to move—if indeed the effort were made. Men stumbled over roots and logs in the woods, or fell in ditches; artillery teams were as ill-humored as their drivers. At last organizations started to move, slowly, and only for a short distance. The unit ahead had halted—or had not yet started. A regiment or a brigade would move again—and halt again. And so it went. A column of 18,000 men, infantry and artillery, bravely on their way to battle, moving along at night, a jerk at a time, wearing themselves out, and dissipating the strength they would need for combat: it was an agonizing sight for their general."

Thus does Kenneth P. Williams describe the march on July 21, 1861, of two divisions of McDowell's army to cover the seven miles from Centerville to Sudley Springs ford. By contrast, after the experience of three years of war, Grant's opening movement into the Wilderness was accomplished without a hitch. His expedition consisted of 120,000 men, 274 field guns, 835 ambulances, 4,300 wagons, 56,499 horses and mules and several thousand head of cattle that were driven along to be slaughtered as needed. In the trains were scores of cannon, caissons and limbers, hundreds of ambulances and thousands of wagons drawn by six-horse teams and loaded with food, forage, ammunition, medical stores, pontoons, tents, and personal baggage of officers.

Sylvanus Cadwallader, a newspaper correspondent who witnessed this tremendous movement, stated that if all the wagons had been arranged close together in a single file the line would have extended from the Rapidan to Petersburg, a distance of more than seventy-five miles. Only the combat trains, carrying the most essential equipment and supplies, accompanied the fighting units. The "great trains," laden with reserves of food, ammunition, and other supplies, came along in the rear or moved by parallel roads.

The Civil War to a large extent was a war of movement. A normal prelude to a battle was a march. In the standard formation infantrymen marched four abreast in a column well closed. Each soldier carried forty to sixty rounds of ammunition and three days' (sometimes more) cooked rations. In the Second Manassas campaign Pope's soldiers carried 100 rounds of ammunition, and on the March to the Sea Sherman's troops carried 40 rounds in the cartridge box and 160 rounds in the haversack. Under normal conditions columns were halted periodically for brief periods of rest. Stonewall Jackson prescribed ten-minute rest intervals every hour and an hour's break at noon. He and most other commanders required that canteens be filled at the beginning of the day and forbade interruption of the march to quench thirst.

Once the column got under way, the men commonly were allowed to relax into "route step" which meant that they marched and carried their weapons in any way they pleased. During the first hour or two there was considerable chatter and chaffing, but as the men settled down to cover the long miles they tended to become less communicative. Some of the marchers found relaxation in singing, but most preferred to plod along in silence.

Before going into action the men were formed in lines of battle. Deployment might be made in a leisurely manner by the marching columns as they arrived at the scene of action. Or, as was the case at Shiloh, the men might be summoned suddenly and unexpectedly from their bivouacs by the "long roll," which was an extended beating of the snare drums.

Normally the infantry was arrayed for battle by brigade, with each brigade formed in two lines, one behind the other. Each line consisted of two ranks separated by about two paces. Composition and arrangement of the lines varied considerably, depending on the size and organization of the force, the nature of the terrain, the preference of the commanding officer and whether or not the role was defense or assault. Frequently the first of the two lines of battle was stronger than the second; in a brigade of five regiments,

Grapevine Bridge over the Chickahominy River, Virginia, Built by the 5th New Hampshire Infantry and by Details from 64th New York and Irish Brigade. Completed, May 29, 1862

United States Engineers Transporting Gun Across River at Fredericksburg, Virginia

three regiments might be placed in the first line and two in the second. But sometimes the two lines were of equal strength, and occasionally the second line was the stronger.

In a large-scale assault, divisions were sometimes formed "in column of brigade," that is, with the brigades (each in two two-rank lines) one behind the other, with intervals of 150 to 300 yards between the brigades. On May 5, 1864, at the Battle of the Wilderness, General James Wadsworth formed his division of four brigades (five regiments to a brigade) for the attack on Ewell thus (— equals one regiment):

In this formation the regiments forming each brigade are in echelon. Sometimes a division commander would form his brigades in echelon:

If a commander wished to increase the depth and power of his attack, he might form his brigades in column of regiments thus:

Longstreet apparently used this formation for the flank attack (with four brigades) made against the Union left at the Wilderness on May 6, 1864. The vulnerability of these dense formations to artillery and rifle fire was clearly demonstrated by the heavy casualties suffered by the Federals at Fredericksburg on December 13, 1862.

An infantry assault was usually preceded by intensive artillery fire, the purpose of which was to cripple opposing guns and prepare the way for the attacking column. When the maximum effects had been achieved by the preparatory fire, the assaulting force, led normally by a thin line of skirmishers whose function was to drive in the enemy pickets and "feel out" the opposition, moved forward in battle formation. At first the attackers encountered relatively light artillery fire, such as could be effectively delivered by the longer-range pieces over the heads of the defending troops. But when the opposing pickets had been driven back to their lines, and the first wave of the assault which by then had absorbed the skirmish line, came within about four hundred yards, the opposing artillery was brought into full play and the pieces charged with canister. The canister fire increased in deadliness as the attackers closed in, cutting huge gaps in their lines. But these holes were quickly filled by the men on the right and left who closed up and "dressed center."

245

Fugitive Negroes Fording the Rappahannock River,
Fleeing from Jackson's Army, August, 1862

Pontoon Boats on Wheels

Lower Pontoon Bridge, Deep Bottom, James River, Virginia, 1865

As the distance between the opposing lines narrowed, the attacking force gradually lost its formation and became a surging mass of yelling individuals. At about two hundred yards muskets were brought into play. Sometimes the first wave of attackers delivered one volley and then rushed on to engage the defenders in hand-to-hand combat. In other instances the men dropped to the ground after delivering their first fire and remained there loading and firing at will until a second wave passed through to push the attack.

Owing to the deadliness of the fire produced by rifled arms, methods of attack were modified as the war progressed. Sometimes entire regiments were deployed as skirmishers, and skirmishers occasionally advanced in such numbers as practically to form a separate line of battle. Intervals between brigades and regiments were increased. More and more, troops scattered for cover and concealment as they came under fire, and thereafter moved forward by intermittent rushes under the cover of fire delivered on the flanks. Even so, these and other tactical developments had only limited application. As a general rule, infantry attacks in the Civil War were made according to conventional eighteenth century modes, with rigidly formed lines moving forward in massive frontal assaults. In the sixties, hostile infantry formed in ranks, shoulder to shoulder, and shot at each other. It was forthright, and it required good stout hearts to stand the ordeal.

These general comments about Civil War tactics have relevancy here chiefly for their bearing on the attitude and conduct of the men who did the fighting.

How did the soldiers feel as they approached the ordeal of battle? Soldiers who had never been under fire joked, laughed, and talked more than those who had "seen the elephant," and veterans were the most reticent of all. George A. Townsend, a newspaper correspondent who accompanied a column of Banks's troops as they approached Cedar Mountain on August 8, 1862, stated: "Many of the soldiers were pensive and thoughtful; but the mass were marching to their funerals with boyish outcries, apparently anxious to forget the responsibilities of the time. . . . A continual explosion of small arms in the shape of epithets, jests, imitations of the cries of sheep, cows, mules and roosters, and snatches of songs enlivened the march." Many of the men observed by Townsend had never been in action before, and the lightheartedness which they displayed was to a large extent feigned to conceal a deep-seated anxiety.

Nervousness increased as the time of commitment approached, and the preliminaries served only to heighten the tension. A common sight as the troops took their places in the line of battle was a stretcher detail huddled about an assistant surgeon for final briefing on the care of the wounded; and occasionally troops marching to their assigned positions were treated to the nerve-racking spectacle of a field hospital staff laying out and sharpening their instruments.

In some instances bands played patriotic airs to inspire the men as they prepared for combat. A Pennsylvania sergeant wrote to his wife that at Cedar Mountain on August 9, 1862, "we went into the field with the Band p[l]aying Dixey." An Ohio soldier who was at Shiloh wrote after the war: "We waited for three quarters of an hour before receiving the command to move. During that time one of the regimental bands played 'Hail Columbia.' It was the first and only time that I heard music on a battlefield, and soon after I saw that heroic band playing 'Over the Hills and Far Away.'"

Forge Scene at Headquarters, Army of the Potomac, Antietam, Maryland, September, 1862

110th Pennsylvania Infantry at Falmouth, Virginia, April 24, 1863, a Few Days Before the Battle of Chancellorsville

Organized in Harrisburg, the regiment went into training, August, 1861. Its battles included Second Manassas, Fredericksburg, Chancellorsville, Gettysburg, Mine Run, the Wilderness Campaign, Battle of the Crater, Hatcher's Run, and the Appomattox Campaign. The regiment lost 7 officers and 111 men killed and mortally wounded and 78 men by disease. The four officers on the left in the front rank are the chaplain, the regimental surgeon, and his two assistant surgeons.

As a general rule the bandsmen dispersed when action commenced so that they could help remove the wounded. But in a few instances commanders insisted that they keep up the music during combat. Brigadier General Horace Porter stated that at Five Forks he encountered one of Major General Phil Sheridan's bands playing "Nellie Bly" under a heavy fire, "as cheerily as if it were furnishing music for a country picnic." And on one great occasion on the first day of Gettysburg the bandsmen of the 20th Maine were ordered to drop their instruments and seize their implements of warfare. "Every pioneer and musician who could carry a musket went into the ranks."

Officers took advantage of the time that usually intervened between the deployment of their units and the disposition of supporting elements to make a final check of weapons and ammunition. A colonel would step to the front of his regiment and make an inspirational address. Some of these speeches were very brief and to the point. Just before committing the Fifth New Hampshire at Antietam, Colonel Cross walked back and forth in front of the formation and said: "Men you are about to engage in battle. You have never disgraced your State; I hope you won't this time. If any man runs I want the file closers to shoot him; if they don't, I shall myself. That's all I have to say." At Fredericksburg, General Thomas F. Meagher, commander of the famous Irish Brigade, according to the report that he made after the fight, "addressed to every regiment separately a few words, reminding them of their duty, and exhorting them to do it bravely and nobly." Before he completed his talk to the last regiment, the unit came under the fire of Confederate artillery and the mangled remains of casualties—"mere masses of blood and rags"—were carried along the line to the rear.

When the time came for the 114th Pennsylvania to go in at Fredericksburg, "Col. [Charles H. T.] Collis took the flag and advancing five paces in front he said waving the flag, 'Now boys is the time to write your names, let every man do his duty, follow me.'" Private A. H. Pickle, who informed his homefolk of the occurrence shortly after the battle, wrote that they did follow him—"and saved our battery and occupied the ground of the rebels." As Collis led his men forward, Pickle observed an incident which would hardly be credible except in the Civil War. In the words of Pickle:

The General [John C. Robinson] rode up to Col. [Andrew H.] Tippin [68th Pennsylvania Regiment] and was about to order him to advance but just as he had the order half uttered he espied a man in Co. D half raised up from his laying position with his open bible in one hand in loud and Earnest prayer. The General stoped a minute until the man closed and put away the book. He said now Col. Tippin advance your men . . . and support Col. Coke's.

To raw soldiers who had never been in battle one of the greatest concerns was whether or not they would be able to meet the awful test of combat. Would they be able to stand unflinching or press on while friends and comrades were struck down on every side. Or would their physical and spiritual powers fail them and cause them to falter or run and bring everlasting disgrace on themselves and their families?

Many were disturbed and depressed by a sense of guilt about their past lives. To most Civil War soldiers God and sin and final judgment were realities, and hell was regarded as the certain lot of those who were found wanting on the day of reckoning. Some who professed godliness were troubled by doubts about the adequacy of their spiritual state, and their whispered supplications were joined with the silent pleas and promises of the avowedly wicked as the formation waited for the order to advance.

Nervousness manifested itself in excessive perspiration, dryness of the lips, heaviness of the chest, and a gnawing emptiness in the area of the stomach. In a few instances the tension proved intolerable. John A. Wyeth who fought with an Alabama regiment at Chickamauga recalled afterward:

As we fell in line for the advance and were loading and capping our guns, a member of my company, pale and trembling, left the line and walked up to the captain. I heard him say, "Captain I cannot go in." Captain James L. Smith . . . replied, more in pity than contempt, "My God, then go back to the horses."

Such cases were unusual. The overwhelming majority silently held their places, but most, if not all, experienced fear in some form or degree. "If you see anyone that says they want any afraid, you know that it want me," wrote a Union private to his sister after Fredericksburg. And the same could have been said by almost any soldier on either side in the wake of any engagement.

When the order to advance finally came, and the men moved out toward their objective, the predominant sensation was one of relief. The terrible waiting was over, and what was to be would quickly be settled. The very act of moving eased their tensions. Nothing that came afterward, except the horrible suffering experienced by the wounded, was as trying as the suspense that preceded the advance.

When the attackers came within range of enemy artillery, some of them instinctively ducked and dodged as the shells whistled close. But officers, by example and by repeating the admonitions, "Steady now," "Center dress," "Close up," helped keep the men in their places. When Grant ordered C. F. Smith to attack the Confederates at Fort Donelson on February 15, 1862, this veteran commander, fully cognizant of the inexperience and nervousness of officers and men, mounted his horse and personally led the advance. His gallantry had the desired effect. One of his soldiers wrote afterward: "I was nearly scared to death, but I saw the old man's white mustache over his shoulder and went on."

Not every officer could write of his men as Jubal Early proudly reported early in 1862 of his brigade: "I have always found it difficult to restrain. It has never been broken or compelled to fall back or left one of its dead to be buried by the enemy." Yet even in this magnificent brigade, surely occasionally a man may have become so demoralized by shell fire that he would drop out of line to seek the protection of a ditch or a tree stump. Such an act if detected would bring a sharp rebuke from his colonel or captain or from the file closers and if words failed to restore him to his place a sabre or a well placed boot would be used. But even with those whose hearts failed in the first supreme test there are many instances after the first wretched minutes, of men who picked up their muskets, ran back into line, and never played the coward again.

On the Union side perhaps the perfect soldier was Captain William Wheeler who wrote home after Gettysburg: "I felt a joyous exultation, a perfect indifference to circumstances, through the whole of that three days' fight, and have seldom enjoyed three days more in my life." His words could be matched by those of a young Virginia soldier going into action for the first time on May 6, 1862. "I did not feel at all afraid, the feeling called fear did not enter my breast but it was a painful, nervous anxiety, a longing for action, anything to occupy my attention. . . . All the energies in my soul, seemed concentrated on the one desire for action. We were not kept long in suspense for very soon orders came for us to go forward."

252

Capture of Fort Harrison by Federal Troops

Battle of Cedar Mountain (Slaughter Mountain) from Point on the Left of the Turnpike

254

255

When the attackers came within musket range, the men received the order to fire. Usually the line was halted for delivery of the first volley, but sometimes the muskets were fired while the ranks were in motion. If a pause was ordered, the men dropped to their knees after firing, or fell to a prone position and rolled over on their backs to reload their guns. Sometimes they loaded and fired several times before resuming the advance. As they bit the end off cartridge after cartridge a layer of black powder accumulated about their lips. But they were too much absorbed in the business at hand to take note of how they looked.

Delivery of the first volley brought further abatement of tension. Raw soldiers were amazed and pleased by the sense of calm that came over them at this stage of the action. "After the first round the fear left me & I was as cool as I ever was in my life," wrote a Union soldier following his initiation into combat. And a Confederate testified after his baptism of fire: "I was a little frightened . . . at first but [soon] . . . became so that I did not care for anything. I fired as cooly as if I had been shooting a squirrel."

But most of the charging men were far less calm than they felt. Many of them were so keyed up with emotion that they failed properly to load and cap their guns after the first fire, and instead of mowing down the enemy as they repeatedly went through the motion of loading, aiming, and firing they simply piled one ball on top of another until musket barrels were gorged with unexploded charges. Of 27,574 guns picked up after Gettysburg, 12,000 contained two charges, 6,000 had from three to ten loads, and one had twenty-three loads. Excitement also manifested itself in vociferous yelling. A Confederate wrote in his diary the day after Gaines's Mill: "We swept forward with wild cheers over

Attempt of Confederates to Recapture Fort Harrison, September 30, 1864

the crest and down the slope . . . our screams sounded like forty thousand wild cats." There was a marked difference between the high-pitched yells with which the Confederates punctuated their assaults and the more uniformly intoned cheers of the Federals. An Ohio sergeant reported after the fight at Mine Run: "The effect of the Enemy's peculiar cheer upon our raw men was very demoralizing. This cheer, or rather hoot, was taken from the Texas Rangers. . . . It is always easy to know which side is advancing by the character of the cheer. Ours was an unmistakable and prolonged hurrah, whilst theirs was a succession of jerky canine yelps, which at a distance from its shrillness seemed like the sound of boys' voices, but when near was terror striking from its savagery."

By no means all of the shouting was done in unison. Once the fighting got under way the tendency was for each man to holler on his own, in accordance with his individual needs and fancies.

As the assault reached the climax the attackers abandoned all pretense of shooting and rushed upon their antagonists with clubbed muskets. (As previously noted, bayonets were hardly ever used.) The defenders responded in kind, and in its final stages the fighting became a frenzied trial of elemental strength, marked by beating, biting, gouging, taunting, and swearing. Presently one side or the other prevailed, and the charge was over. Other charges and countercharges might follow before the outcome of the battle was decided, but all of them followed the same general pattern.

What was a battle like? One feature vividly remembered by participants was the pandemonium. The din of combat was more than a figure of speech. "I have never heard such a noise in all my life," wrote a Georgian after Chancellorsville; and an Arkansas captain who

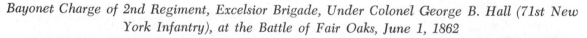

Bayonet Charge of 2nd Regiment, Excelsior Brigade, Under Colonel George B. Hall (71st New York Infantry), at the Battle of Fair Oaks, June 1, 1862

Death of a Soldier, Battle of Hatcher's Run

Portrait of a Child Found on the Battlefield at Port Republic by Thomas W. Timberlake, 2nd Virginia Infantry, Between the Bodies of a Federal Soldier and a Confederate Soldier

was at Murfreesboro stated: "I cannot use language to Express the nois of this Battle. The Earth seemed to be in perfect commotion as if a heavy Earth Quake was on. . . . It seemed as if the Heavens and Earth had broke loose." A Virginia private who helped repel the Federal attack near Petersburg on June 18, 1864, reported to his brother: "You Couldent hear your own gun Shoot the Canon was roaring bumb shells bursting, bullets whistling, men hollowing."

Another feature of combat which stuck in the minds of participants was the confusion. Frank Aretas Haskell recalled Antietam as "A great tumbling together of all heaven and earth." Some engagements were more orderly than others, of course. But in most big battles, and especially those fought in rough or wooded terrain, units became hopelessly commingled, and individuals and small groups eventually fought pretty much on their own. After Chancellorsville, Brigadier General Alfred Iverson reported that his and Brigadier General Colston's lines merged during the fighting "and caused great confusion . . . rushing forward pellmell upon the enemy and becoming mingled in almost inextricable confusion, no officer being able to tell what men he commanded." The same could have been said by many commanders after Shiloh, the two Manassas battles, the Wilderness, and almost any other large engagement.

A battle was an extremely exhausting experience, and the weariness lingered on in the minds of participants. A Minnesota soldier who had been accustomed to strenuous exertion in civilian life wrote shortly after First Manassas: "it was the hardest day's work I ever expect to do." A New Englander informed his homefolk after an engagement near Petersburg in June, 1864, that "nothing is so tiresome as fighting." Soldiers were often aroused long before daylight when a battle was in prospect and subjected to several hours of marching and suspense before their actual commitment. The anxiety produced by the waiting was hardly less enervating than the fighting that followed. Little wonder that soldiers had to pause now and then "to blow" as they rushed forward to engage the foe. At the conclusion of a day of fighting such as April 6, 1862, at Shiloh, September 17, 1862, at Antietam, or May 6, 1864, at the Wilderness men would sometimes fall down in their tracks into a sleep so deep that comrades could walk over their prostrate forms without waking them.

Shiloh, Antietam, Fredericksburg, Chancellorsville, Gettysburg, Chickamauga, Spotsylvania, and Second Cold Harbor were terrible carnages. At Balaklava, in the charge immortalized by Tennyson, the Light Brigade suffered casualties in killed and wounded of 36.7 per cent. But in the Civil War, 115 regiments—63 Union and 52 Confederate—sustained losses of more than 50 per cent in a single engagement. At Antietam 82.3 per cent of the officers and men of the First Texas Regiment were killed or wounded. At Gettysburg the First Minnesota Regiment lost 82 per cent, and the Twenty-sixth North Carolina, which claimed to have suffered greater losses than any other regiment on either side in any Civil War battle, reported 100 per cent casualties in Company F on the first day; and Company E, the other center company, which went into action that morning with 82 officers and men, concluded the day's fighting with only two alive and unharmed.

The enormous spilling of blood made a profound impression on those who had a part in it. A Confederate wrote after a bloody assault in the Wilderness in May, 1864: "We charged them out of 2 lines of breastwork and drove them back 3 miles. And as the saying

Dead Confederate Soldier, Fort Mahone, Petersburg, Virginia

Dr. Bunnell's Embalming Establishment in the Field near Fredericksburg, Virginia

Soldier's Grave in Front of House on Fair Oaks Battlefield

"Here and there, you come on a little ridge of earth, marked by a bit of board, on which is scrawled the name of the soldier, who lies where he fell, in this desert region. Our people are very different from the Europeans in their care for the dead, and mark each grave with its name; even in the heat of battle."

is, we made a hog killing business of it." An Ohio soldier who walked over the field of Antietam two days after the fight described the scene thus to his father:

The smell was offul . . . their was about 5 or 6,000 dead bodes decaying over the field and perhaps 100 dead horses . . . their lines of battle Could be run for miles by the dead they lay long the lines like sheavs of Wheat I could have walked on the boddes all most from one end too the other.

After Gettysburg a Maine soldier wrote to his parents: "I have Seen . . . men rolling in their own blood, Some Shot one place, Some another. . . . our dead lay in the road and the Rebels in their hast to leave dragged both their baggage wagons and artillery over them and they lay mangled and torn to pieces so that Even friends could not tell them. You can form no idea of a battle field . . . no pen can describe it. No tongue can tell its horror I hope none of my brothers will Ever have to go into a fight."

Horror and tragedy found most vivid expression in individual instances observed by the soldiers. At Milliken's Bend, and on several other battlefields, pairs of opposing soldiers were found lying close together, each transfixed by the bayonet of the other. At New Hope Church in May, 1864, three Confederate brothers were killed in succession as they rammed charges into one of the guns of Fenner's battery; and after this fight a Confederate walking over the field found two boys in blue, obviously twins about fifteen years old, lying dead with their hands clasped. After Seven Pines a New Yorker wrote to his homefolk: "I saw a [Confederate] Father & Son side by side wounded. They both died where they lay." A Confederate colonel in recounting the experience of the Fifth Texas Regiment at Gettysburg stated: "There were two twin brothers belonging to Company C . . . [who] came up to where I was standing and commenced firing. In a moment one of them is shot down by my side. The other brother caught hold of him as he fell and gently laid him down on the ground, and as he did so, he also received a death shot."

When Jeff Forrest, Nathan Bedford Forrest's brother, was killed in a charge near Okolona, Mississippi, in 1864, Nathan dismounted from his horse, took his dead brother in his arms, kissed him tenderly and then, according to the captain who reported the incident, "springing to his horse he called on us to follow him." Equally touching was a similar tragedy experienced by General Wade Hampton at Hatcher's Run on October 27, 1864. When one son, Preston, was shot from his horse, another son, Wade, dismounted to aid him. As young Wade stooped to examine his brother, he himself was struck down by an enemy bullet. Just then General Hampton came up and swung out of his saddle. Perceiving that young Wade's wound was relatively slight and Preston's mortal, he gathered the dying boy in his arms, muttered, "My son, my son," kissed him, whispered words of comfort into his ear, and with tears streaming down his bearded face committed both boys to the care of other officers and rode forward to battle.

One of the heroes was Jere S. Gage of Company A, the University Greys, Eleventh Mississippi Regiment. Jere left the University of Mississippi Law School in the spring of 1861 and passed safely through the early battles in Virginia (though he counted seventeen bullet holes in his clothes after Seven Pines). He was seriously wounded at Gaines's Mill but recovered sufficiently to accompany his unit to Gettysburg. He was struck down by a shell on the third day and taken to a field hospital. When Dr. Joseph Holt, the regimental

Burying the Dead

"It takes a lot of glory out of war to see the dead being buried. They would dig a ditch 6 feet wide, 2 feet deep and as long as was necessary, and would lay the poor boys, side by side, head to feet every other row, put their hat or cap down over the face and cover them up, putting a bit of board at each head with a number on it, to save the record."—John F. Campbell who, as a boy on his father's farm, witnessed the Battle of Stones River.

Graves of Confederate Soldiers in Hollywood Cemetery, Richmond, Virginia

"There is no holier spot of ground
Than where defeated valor lies."
—Henry Timrod

surgeon, came to examine him he offered words of comfort about the left arm which was torn off at the elbow.

"Why, Doctor, that is nothing," said the wounded man; "here is where I am really hurt," and he turned back his blanket to reveal a horrible wound in his abdomen.

"Doctor, how long have I to live?" asked Gage.

"A very few hours," replied the surgeon.

"Doctor, I am in great agony; let me die easy, dear doctor," muttered the patient.

Fortunately the surgeon had at hand some opium which he diluted in water; but before handing the cup to Gage he asked, "Have you no message to leave?"

"My mother . . . Quick! I want to write," replied the suffering man.

Pen and paper were immediately obtained, and with the doctor supporting him the patient wrote a few farewell words to his mother. The letter finished, he drank the opiate, returned the cup to the doctor with a "Thank you," and settled down into his last long sleep.

Over in the Federal lines on that same terrible third day at Gettysburg was a young battery commander, Lieutenant A. H. Cushing. During the heavy artillery fire preceding and accompanying Pickett's assault, all but one of Cushing's guns were disabled. While directing the fire of the one remaining piece, Cushing's stomach was torn open by a Confederate shell. Fully aware of the crisis which then imperiled the Union, Cushing held his intestines in place with one hand and with the other helped push the gun forward to a more advantageous position. As the gun was wheeled in place Cushing cried out to his general, "I will give them one more shot!" Then, when the charge had sped on its way, he shouted, "Goodbye," and fell lifeless across the cannon.

Many of the most resplendent feats of valor were performed by the common soldiers of both sides. The Civil War was a soldier's war. Officer casualties were heavy; and those who survived in the hurly-burly of combat often were able to exercise little control over their units. In the crucial, climactic stages of battle the common soldiers had to make their own decisions, and their resourcefulness, tenacity, and courage were what counted most in deciding the outcome. They who fought there, whether at Manassas, Gettysburg, or Bentonville, were the bedrock of their respective causes, and their greatness helped to make their war one of the most inspiring in the history of embattled humanity.

Colonel Roy Stone, who commanded a brigade of three Pennsylvania regiments at Gettysburg, had this to say of his command: "No language can do justice to the conduct of my officers and men on the bloody 'first day'; to the coolness with which they watched and waited, under a fierce storm of shot and shell, the approach of the enemy's overwhelming masses; [to] their ready obedience to orders, and the prompt and perfect execution, under fire, of all the tactics of the battle-field; to the fierceness of their repeated attacks; or to the desperate tenacity of their resistance. They fought as if each man felt that upon his own arm hung the fate of the day and the nation. Nearly two-thirds of my command fell on the field. Every field officer save one was wounded and disabled."

Joseph C. Stiles, a distinguished minister who accompanied Lee's army on the Antietam campaign, wrote afterward to his daughter: "I could tell you a thousand thrilling incidents indicative of the glorious courage of our soldiers." After the battle of Chickamauga a Confederate brigade commander, William B. Bate, reported: "The private soldier . . . [vied] with the officer in deeds of high daring and distinguished courage. While the 'River of Death' shall float its sluggish current to the beautiful Tennessee, and the night wind chant its solemn dirges over their soldier graves, their names, enshrined in the hearts of their countrymen, will be held in grateful remembrance."

In his official report of the Murfreesboro campaign, General W. S. Rosecrans, after noting the splendid conduct of officers, stated: "But, above all, the sturdy rank and file showed invincible fighting courage and stamina, worthy of a great and free nation." A few days after Rosecrans had made his report, Braxton Bragg, the commander who had opposed him at Murfreesboro, wrote to the Confederate adjutant general:

In the absence of the instruction and discipline of old armies . . . we have had in a great measure to trust to the individuality and self-reliance of the private soldier. Without the incentive or the motive which controls the officer, who hopes to live in history; without the hope of reward, and actuated only by a sense of duty and of patriotism, he has, in this great contest, justly judged that the cause was his own, and gone into it with a determination to conquer or die. . . . No encomium is too high, no honor too great for such a soldiery. However much of credit and glory may be given . . . the leaders in our struggle, history will yet award the main honor where it is due—to the private soldier, who . . . has encountered all the hardships and suffered all the privations.

Bragg's prediction that history would award principal honor to the private soldier has not yet been borne out. The generals and political leaders as subjects continue to dominate writings about the Civil War. But Bragg was right in his appraisal of the character of the Confederate private. And what he said about the Southerner's self-reliance and dependability was equally applicable to the man who wore the blue.

A word that occurs again and again in contemporary writing by the soldiers on both sides is "valor," not "bravery" or "courage" or "gallantry," but "valor." No greater tribute was paid the common soldier of both armies than General Taliaferro's words when he described the deadly encounter between the Iron Brigade and Jackson's men at Manassas Junction on August 28, 1862:

"It was a stand-up combat, dogged and unflinching, in a field almost bare. . . . There was cover of woods not very far in rear of the lines on both sides, and brave men . . . might have been justified in seeking this shelter from the iron hail that smote them; but out in the sunlight, in the dying daylight, and under the stars, they stood, and although they could not advance, they would not retire. There was some discipline in this, but there was much more of true valor . . . it was a question of endurance, and both endured."

United States Military Asylum Cemetery, Washington, D.C.

This cemetery was established at Soldiers' Home, Washington, D.C., on July 25, 1861. The first burial was on August 1, 1861. On May 12, 1864, the cemetery was completely filled with 5,211 graves. Later, the name of the cemetery was changed to Soldiers' Home National Cemetery.

Picture Credits

CHAPTER I

2 Mrs. Ruby F. R. Thomas and Georgia State Department of Archives and History, Atlanta, Ga.

6 Ambrotype. Collection, Mr. Elmer O. Parker, Washington, D. C.

8 Ambrotype. Collection, Mr. Lee Grove, New York, N. Y.

8 Ambrotype. Collection, Mrs. Linda Cudé, Washington, D. C.

9 Confederate Museum, Richmond, Va.

9 Ambrotype. Collection, Mrs. Linda Cudé, Washington, D. C.

10 Ambrotype. Confederate Museum, Richmond, Va.

13 Ambrotype. Collection, Judge William Finley, Falls Church, Va.

14 Tintype. Logan Collection, Illinois State Historical Library, Springfield, Ill.

15 Ambrotype. Logan Collection, Illinois State Historical Library, Springfield, Ill.

17 John Jex Bardwell. Burton Historical Collection, Detroit Public Library., Detroit, Mich.

CHAPTER II

20 John Jex Bardwell. Burton Historical Collection, Detroit Public Library, Detroit, Mich.

24 National Archives.

25 National Archives.

27 Pencil drawing by C. J. Iwansky. Library of Congress.

29 National Archives.

31 Wash drawing by Alfred R. Waud. Library of Congress.

31 J. D. Edwards, New Orleans, La. Library of Congress.

33 National Archives.

34 National Archives.

35 National Archives.

36 National Archives.

37 Library of Congress.

39 National Archives.

40 National Archives.

41 National Archives.

43 Chromolithograph by M. and N. Hanhart, 1871, after a painting by Conrad Wise Chapman. Library of Congress.

44 George N. Barnard. National Archives.

45 National Archives.

CHAPTER III

48 Library of Congress.

52 Smithsonian Institution.

53 T. H. O'Sullivan. Library of Congress.

55 National Archives.

56 Drawing by Frank Vizetelly of the *Illustrated London News.* Harvard College Library.

57 T. H. O'Sullivan. Library of Congress.

59 James Gardner. Library of Congress.

60 National Archives.

61 James F. Gibson. Library of Congress.

62 T. H. O'Sullivan. Library of Congress.

65 Pencil drawing by Alfred R. Waud. Library of Congress.

CHAPTER IV

68 National Archives.

72 Kepis, collection, Mr. John L. Rawls, Vienna, Va.

72 Buckles, Manassas National Battlefield Park, Manassas, Va.

73 Mathew B. Brady. Library of Congress.

76 Alexander Gardner. Library of Congress.

78 T. H. O'Sullivan. Library of Congress.

82 Ambrotype. Confederate Museum, Richmond, Va.

82 Tintype. Missouri Historical Society, St. Louis, Mo.

83 Ambrotype. Mr. Milton T. Chambers, Baltimore, Md.

85 Library of Congress.

86 Mathew B. Brady. Brady-Handy Collection, Library of Congress.

87 Library of Congress.

88 Ambrotype. Logan Collection, Illinois State Historical Library, Springfield, Ill.

88 National Archives.

88 Mathew B. Brady. Library of Congress.

89 National Archives.

90 Federal canteen, Fredericksburg and Spotsylvania National Military Park, Fredericksburg, Va.

90 Confederate canteen, collection, Mr. John L. Rawls, Vienna, Va.

90 Confederate shoes, Confederate Museum, Charleston, S. C.

90 Federal shoes, Smithsonian Institution.

91 Confederate Museum, Richmond, Va.

93 Mathew B. Brady. Library of Congress.

94 T. H. O'Sullivan. Library of Congress.

95 T. H. O'Sullivan. Library of Congress.

96 Confederate Museum, Richmond, Va.

97 Confederate Museum, Richmond, Va.

98 Samuel A. Cooley. Library of Congress.

99 Smithsonian Institution.

CHAPTER V

102 Captain Andrew J. Russell. Library of Congress.

106 Pencil drawing. Library of Congress.

108 Smithsonian Institution.

109 Smithsonian Institution.

110 Smithsonian Institution.

110 West Point Museum Collection.

110 Collection, Mr. John L. Rawls, Vienna, Va.

111 Mr. Thomas Spencer, Atlanta, Ga.

111 West Point Museum Collection.

113 Smithsonian Institution.

115 Mathew B. Brady, Illinois State Historical Library, Springfield, Ill.

116 Collection, Mr. John L. Rawls, Vienna, Va.

117 Library of Congress.

118 Smithsonian Institution.

119 Confederate Museum, Richmond, Va.

120 Mathew B. Brady. Brady-Handy Collection, Library of Congress.

122 Fredericksburg and Spotsylvania National Military Park, Fredericksburg, Va.

122 Tar Bucket, Manassas National Battlefield Park, Manassas, Va.

123 Fredericksburg and Spotsylvania National Military Park, Fredericksburg, Va.

124 T. H. O'Sullivan. Library of Congress.

127 Library of Congress.

128 James F. Gibson. Library of Congress.

130 James F. Gibson. Library of Congress.

131 David Knox. Library of Congress.

132 Library of Congress.

133 James F. Gibson. Library of Congress.

134 Library of Congress.

136 Library of Congress.

137 S. R. Seibert. Library of Congress.

139 Library of Congress.

CHAPTER VI

142 Pencil drawing by Edwin Forbes. Library of Congress.

145 Pencil drawing by Alfred R. Waud. Library of Congress.

147 Mathew B. Brady. Library of Congress.

148 Alexander Gardner. Library of Congress.

150 Pencil drawing by Alfred R. Waud. Library of Congress.

152 James F. Gibson or James Gardner. Library of Congress.

152 Library of Congress.

153 Library of Congress.

155 Drawing by Frank Vizetelly. Harvard College Library.

156 Mathew B. Brady. Library of Congress.

157 Pencil drawing by Edwin Forbes. Library of Congress.

159 National Archives.

160 Alexander Gardner. Library of Congress.

CHAPTER VII

164 T. H. O'Sullivan. Library of Congress.
168 T. H. O'Sullivan. Library of Congress.
171 James Gardner. Library of Congress.
172 Pencil drawing by Edwin Forbes. Library of Congress.
176 Pencil drawing by Alfred R. Waud. Library of Congress.

179 Pencil drawing by Alfred R. Waud. Library of Congress.
180 Pencil drawing by Alfred R. Waud. Library of Congress.
183 Fredericksburg and Spotsylvania National Military Park, Fredericksburg, Va.
185 Haas and Peale. Chicago Historical Society, Chicago, Ill.

CHAPTER VIII

188 Wood and Gibson. National Archives.
193 Mathew B. Brady. Library of Congress.
196 Mathew B. Brady. Library of Congress.

200 Mathew B. Brady. Library of Congress.
203 Library of Congress.
205 Mathew B. Brady. Library of Congress.

CHAPTER IX

208 James Gardner or William M. Smith. Library of Congress.
212 T. H. O'Sullivan. Library of Congress.
213 Wash drawing by William Waud. Library of Congress.
214 National Archives.
216 Ambrotype. Confederate Museum, Richmond, Va.
217 Ambrotype. Confederate Museum, Richmond, Va.
219 Library of Congress.

222 T. H. O'Sullivan. Library of Congress.
224 Confederate Museum, Richmond, Va.
227 Fredericksburg and Spotsylvania National Military Park, Fredericksburg, Va.
228 Mathew B. Brady. National Archives.
229 Mathew B. Brady. National Archives.
231 Mathew B. Brady. Library of Congress.
233 James Gardner. Library of Congress.
234 James Gardner. Brady-Handy Collection, Library of Congress.
237 Library of Congress.

CHAPTER X

240 Painting by Gilbert Gaul. Reproduced by permission of the owner, Mr. John E. Meyer.
243 D. B. Woodbury. Library of Congress.
244 National Archives.
246 T. H. O'Sullivan. Library of Congress.
246 Library of Congress.
247 National Archives.
249 Captain Andrew J. Russell. Library of Congress.
250 Alexander Gardner. Library of Congress.
253 Pencil drawing by William Waud. Library of Congress.
254 Pencil drawing by Edwin Forbes. Library of Congress.

256 Pencil and wash drawing by William Waud. Library of Congress.
257 Pencil drawing by Alfred R. Waud. Library of Congress.
258 Pencil drawing by Sergeant C. W. Reed. Library of Congress.
259 Ambrotype. Confederate Museum, Richmond, Va.
261 Library of Congress.
262 Library of Congress.
263 James F. Gibson. Library of Congress.
265 National Archives.
266 Library of Congress.
269 Library of Congress.